# Contents

# Contents

# Introduction

I was almost bankrupt, I was exhausted, and I was about to call it quits in 2009—two years after starting my first business. Like most new entrepreneurs, my business partner and I had rolled up our sleeves and started to work in the business immediately. We did that for two long awful years and it nearly cost us everything. Ironically it was a huge break from a national retailer that forced my partner and me to stop and think about the business. It forced us to analyze and reflect on what we were doing and how poorly we were doing it. It made us realize we had to change our mindset. We had to change our habits and our frantic pace. That retailer helped us stop and push the reset button, which led to an amazing transformation in us and in the business.

Chances are if you are an entrepreneur, you've found yourself in a similar situation, feeling overwhelmed, and not knowing which direction you should be headed in. That's why I wrote this book. *The Entrepreneur's Book of Actions* will help you lead better, think better, work differently and more focused, and ultimately find the success you want. And it breaks the process down into manageable steps that you can build on each day. It will help you develop what I call "the success mindset." The book will help you approach your business with a sense of clarity and purpose.

Let's face it, the days of unrelenting brand loyalty that companies like Sears and McDonald's once enjoyed is forever buried in our past. They've been replaced with a much younger, more sophisticated generation armed with smartphones and apps that give us instant information.

· In fact, there is only one way for you to compete as an entrepreneur in this new world and that is a personal evolution. You must evolve into a stronger, smarter, more resilient business leader. You have to thrill your customers. Inspire your staff. Seize opportunity and never stop growing.

Think of your business like a well-trained muscle. If you ignore it, it will experience atrophy, becoming weak and unable to do even the simplest of tasks. If you work it out every day, it will be strong and healthy. That's what makes this book different. It is the first daily exercise manual for your business where you work at making changes and creating better habits every day for a whole year.

Let's talk for a moment about what this book is and what it's not. I have designed it to give you the tools to improve both yourself and your business, but know that it will take daily practice and serious commitment to find lasting success. Each lesson by itself is a building block, one small piece of the puzzle, in what it takes to become a complete business leader. So I want you to know this book is not one that you can read in a few days and expect miraculous transformations. In other words, this is not a "quick fix" book.

If your goal is to find inspiration and creativity and to define what success really means for you, then this book will give you the necessary tools to make those discoveries. It will also teach you to better manage your life, your business, and your relationships, plus create a team of motivated employees and loyal customers.

This book is a daily devotional and it is designed to take 53 weeks to complete. From my life experience the kind of significant change you seek takes time and commitment. Habits are hard to change. Creating new ones is even harder.

The entire blueprint is here and ready for you to learn from.

Each day you will be asked to complete an exercise that will help you focus on bringing out the very best qualities of the leader and person inside of you. This daily devotional will free your soul as you learn, relearn, and master these principles. You will be amazed when you start to realize how much your company will change over the next 53 weeks.

If you take each devotion to heart as you embark on this life-changing journey, then I can make you three promises right here and now:

**1.** You'll get to know yourself better than you ever have before.
**2.** Your business relationships will become stronger than ever.
**3.** You'll be happier, more confident, and a much better leader.

With that, I can only offer one final piece of advice. As you devote your time to learning and practicing these new techniques, be sure to be brutally honest with yourself. That's easy for me to say, but doing it is quite another thing altogether. Trust me when I say this: The hardest truths to admit are often the most liberating once they're truly acknowledged. So don't sell yourself short; dig deep and look for the answers from within.

Before you turn the page and start with Week 1, go out and purchase a brand-new notebook to serve as a daily journal. Each day, you'll be given a brief assignment and then you'll be asked to write a few words about it. I cannot stress how critically important writing down your thoughts are for this process to work, and you will access this notebook frequently.

Are you ready to make real lasting change in your life and in your business? Then it is time for you to prove it by your *actions*. You can read this book a million times, but if you do not take action and practice the lessons that the book teaches, you will not progress in your business. So, let's get started on this journey together! Today is the first day of your transformation.

# THE
# ENTREPRENEUR'S
# BOOK OF
# ACTIONS

# Passion and Purpose

Welcome to the first of 53 weeks that will help you change yourself and your business for the better. Before you begin to decide exactly what you need to do to grow and create the life you've always dreamed of, let's go back to the beginning.

Where did it all start? Discovering your purpose in life is where you find fulfillment and satisfaction. Do you remember what you wanted to be the first time someone asked you?

No, I don't mean when your response was a fireman or a princess. I mean when you had a real, honest answer that was fueled by passion. Try to remember that feeling. If you can put that feeling into who you are as an entrepreneur today, then you'll be off to a great start.

## DAY 1

> *I have a purpose. I may be making a living, but I also have a life to live. It is my purpose to find a way to do both in the best possible way!*

### Finding Your Purpose

Your purpose is what gets you out of bed in the morning and makes time fly. But have you discovered your purpose? How and when did you know?

If you don't know, then why is it important to find your purpose? How do you go about finding it? Some people seem to be born knowing what brings joy and meaning to them. Most of us, however, need to figure it out for ourselves.

Before we start asking ourselves some very important questions, let's begin with what we already know. Make a list of what you feel your purpose is, what your company's purpose is, and what your purpose within the company is. Are they the same? Spend some time today thinking about exactly what led you to this point.

## DAY 2

> *My why will define my how! I will do what makes me happy and learn how to do it in a way that will support my dreams.*

### Ask the Right Questions

Each day this week you are going to ask yourself a question and write down the answer. Place that answer somewhere that you will see it throughout the day and constantly dwell on it as you progress through the day.

Today we will start with this one. Ask yourself, "What makes me feel happy and alive?"

This question has nothing to do with your business. Your purpose is often related to what you love to do; it may or may not be connected to your actual career. You may find it while volunteering or in your favorite hobby . . . or it can be something completely different.

Think about what you look forward to, and consider how you can expand those activities into more of your life. In one word, write down your purpose and stick it where you will see it often throughout the day. Remember, your purpose is not a goal, it's what's driving your toward the goals that we will talk about later.

Write down the things that make you feel happy and alive. Try to do at least one of those things today.

## DAY 3

> *My future is bright! I will find my purpose*
> *and use it to define my future.*

### Find Your Good

Today you need to dig deep inside and be a little bit arrogant. Ask yourself, "What am I good at?"

Don't be so humble! We all have talents and skills. What are yours? You may have the ability to build things, the patience to be a mentor or the vision of a leader. You'll find more success in using natural strengths than in trying to get rid of your self-perceived weaknesses. Today, write down what you are good at and place it next to your purpose. Do they coincide? Does what you are good at change what you feel about your purpose? Make sure that you see the words often and spend time meditating over how you feel about them. Try to envision where they fit into your life right now.

## DAY 4

> *I will not let others take away my joy! I will*
> *not let someone else define my happiness.*

### Don't Show Me the Money

We all know that money is necessary for survival. But what if it weren't? What if you could do anything and not worry about money at all? Dream a little today and ask yourself, "If income didn't matter, what would I be doing?"

This question often leads directly to the discovery of your purpose, which means that the answer can point you in the direction of finding true happiness. So it's an important one to consider.

Write down the answer and place it next to your answers to Days 1 and 2. Has anything changed?

If the answer to this question changes your purpose, then ask yourself, "Was I being brutally honest on Day 1?" Really believe that this kind of freedom is possible, and take your purpose—what you are good at—and turn it into the money you need to survive. Don't let yourself get stuck; start taking small steps to reach your goal.

## DAY 5

> *Today I will take it one step at a time. Small accomplishments will be huge assets in my life.*

### Be the Good

I truly believe that somewhere inside of each and every one of us, we want to make the world a better place. Yes, some of you have those narcissistic tendencies that might put yourself first, and that's fine, but there's still that hope for the greater good somewhere instinctively inside of you.

Today, ask yourself, "How can I add greater value to the world?"

Does your purpose help you to do this? If not directly, then how can the success of your purpose help you to add greater value to the world? Write down your hopes to make the world a better place today and place that note next to your other notes. Then take an extra moment today and look at your answers.

Imagine how you might feel if you were living your life with all of these things in it. When you take time to become self-aware, you can see where to use your knowledge and skills. You may be passionate about helping the elderly, building a new playground for the neighborhood, or changing laws in your city. Each of us has unique interests that can be used to make the world a better place.

## DAY 6

> *Anyone can change the world. Today*
> *I will figure out how to do it.*

### Leave Your Mark

Now that you realize your purpose and how it fits in with what you are good at, ask yourself, "What will be my legacy?" What do you want to be remembered for? What do you want to leave behind? Your purpose in life can affect how you will be remembered; it's an opportunity to leave your mark in the world and to make a positive difference in the lives of others.

Now, take a step back. Today's exercise will be difficult.

Write down what your legacy will be if you don't make a change today—if you don't focus on your purpose and do what you are good at. What will you be remembered for if you never push yourself to be anything more than you are today?

Write your legacy down and keep it separate from your other notes. Hang it up so that you can see it at various times throughout your day, especially when you need some inspiration! Take in exactly how that makes you feel.

## DAY 7

> *I have a legacy to build. My legacy will be outstanding!*
> *Today is the first day in the book of my life.*

### The Time Is Now

When you begin to consider your purpose, you are on your way to the happiness and enthusiasm that will enrich your life and the lives of others. You will have a natural focus that will drive you to reach your goals—you will become successful, on your own terms. Why not start today?

Now, let's go back to that legacy that we talked about yesterday. Write down exactly how you want to be remembered and what it will be for. Be completely honest and do it with the hopes that all of the other things you've written down the first five days of this week have come to fruition.

How does it make you feel? Can you push those awful feelings from yesterday away and step into the second week of taking control of your business and your life? YES! You are ready to start growing!

# Stepping-Stones

A recent online post I read shared a three-step program that anyone can use to motivate himself or herself. Wow, just three easy steps to significant change. Sounds simple, right? Wrong.

It takes work. It takes commitment. But if you start today by finding your motivation and sticking to it, you will be on the road to building a successful business and a happy life in less than a year.

So, the question arises: How do you motivate yourself? Write down the things that you do to motivate yourself. Maybe you have a song that gets you pumped up or a verse that you repeat to yourself. Maybe you think about your family. Whatever it is that you think is your motivation, make a note of it. If you don't already have one, I would like you to start a journal where you can keep your thoughts organized. Then you can use it throughout this process and go back and see how you have grown by the time you reach the end.

Take up an entire page doodling about the things that motivate you. Make it artistic and explosive; decorate your words. Remind yourself of those motivations every time you look at the doodling.

## DAY 1

> *My mood will not be my master. Today I will try to control my mood and refuse to allow it to control me.*

## A Positive Attitude Equals Success

The first step is to assume a positive, optimistic attitude. Research suggests that we procrastinate more frequently when we're in a sour mood. This fact brings forth another question: How do we find positive energy when we're not feeling very good?

Make a list of things that put you in a bad mood. Think about how those things directly affect your motivation to succeed within your business. Dwell on those things today and try to decide if they really matter in your world.

## DAY 2

*Opportunities can be found! Today is a treasure trove full of them and I am going to begin to check them off my list now!*

## My To-Do Today

One problem with finding motivation is that many people make to-do lists, but not many people force themselves to get the items on the list done. The reason is that we use our ability to think to figure out what needs to be done, but actually doing them requires motivation and focus.

Today, make your own to-do list just for this week. Focus on things that you are avoiding on a daily basis and find the opportunity to resolve those issues.

Next, think of why you want to reach those goals in one word. Find a smooth stone from your garden or on a nearby road and write the word on that rock or make a small sign to keep in your office or to place on your bathroom mirror. Place it anywhere that will remind you of your first step in a new direction.

## DAY 3

> *There are things that I need to stop doing. Today I will try to stop at least one in order to make my life better.*

### Take a Step Back

Before you reach step two, let's stop for a moment and look back at your list. How did yesterday go? Did you accomplish at least one thing on the list? What stopped you from accomplishing everything? Yes, time for another list.

Write down what stopped you. Was it the same things that were blocking your motivation? How is your attitude?

Make a list of things that you need to stop doing in order to accomplish your to-do list. Then put that list somewhere you will see it every day, like the wallpaper on your phone. Read it over and over again until you despise the things that are holding you back.

## DAY 4

> *I believe in myself. The rewards of victory will be a prize of immeasurable proportions!*

### Reward Yourself

Once you've learned what's stopping you from finding your motivation, you can move on to the second step—reward yourself when you've completed a necessary task. This tactic can be as simple as having a dessert at dinner or seeing a favorite movie.

Today, make sure that you reward yourself as though you were a child learning a new task. Talk to yourself about your successes; be sure you are recognizing your own accomplishments, no matter how small they may be. Then make a note about what your reward was and how you felt when you achieved it.

## DAY 5

> *There are consequences to my actions. If I fail, I*
> *will accept those consequences with honor.*

### Pop Quiz!

Now that you've learned to reward yourself when you stick to finding your motivation and accomplishing your goals, were you more successful? Or did you struggle? Even though it may have worked out well, now you need to test yourself.

Here's an idea that could cost you if you don't persevere. Find a friend that you trust and give him or her $100 with the goal of sticking to your to-do list for the entire day. If you complete the tasks, at the end of the day, you get the $100 back. If you fail to complete the tasks, your friend keeps the money. See what you learn when you hold yourself accountable and motivate yourself with a possible reward and possible punishment.

## DAY 6

> *Other people's happiness will not define my*
> *happiness! I will not spend my time and energy*
> *trying to make other people happy.*

### Find Your Happy People

The last step is to surround yourself with people who will encourage you to get things done. Peer pressure has gotten a bad rap because of its tendency to cause kids to do inappropriate things, but peer pressure can also become an incredibly positive influence in our lives. There is nothing quite as inspiring as having the right types of friends who are successful and who motivate you through example.

Write down a list of people who motivate you, and also a list of those who bring you down. Find a way to work your world around those positive personalities and make them more prominent within your life. It may be difficult to cut out friends who are holding you back, but try to at least avoid them until your major tasks are accomplished. Negativity is a virus that will overtake your motivation . . . if you let it.

## DAY 7

> *I refuse to wait until I am dead to reap the rewards that I've earned in this lifetime! I will seize the day.*

### The To-Don't List

Now it's time to look at your negative friends list and prove each of them wrong. Cast those doubters aside and focus solely on your motivation. Did you find it this week? If not, then keep looking—it will be critical for your personal and professional successes.

For today's exercise, write a list of the things holding you back from achieving your goals. We will call it your "to-don't" list. These could be skills that you do not have or bad habits that you waste far too much time and energy on. Then moving forward, revisit your "to-don't" list as often as your to-do list to ensure that you are keying in on the proper focus.

# Mental Motivation

Each time you face a fear and overcome it, you gain great strength. One of the ironic things about fear is that it becomes a mental obstacle for most people, causing them to be less of the person they could be in life. In other words, it stops them from accomplishing great things. I believe this lies at the root of much of the abject frustration that exists in the world today.

## DAY 1

> *My fears do not control my life. I will not listen to them! I will be the person that I am destined to be.*

### Breaking Down Fear

It's important to start by understanding that significant fear cannot be overcome overnight. That's why it's significant. To effectively deal with this kind of fear, it's helpful to break down the object of your fear into small, more manageable chunks.

For example, if you're scheduled to give some sort of presentation to a group but have great fear that you'll make a mess of it, break the task down as follows:

1. Know the subject matter to be covered.
2. Develop the actual content of the presentation.
3. Create the materials to be handed out to attendees.

**4.** Scout the venue.

**5.** Visualize the successful presentation.

**6.** Rehearse the presentation to yourself.

**7.** Rehearse the presentation to a group and solicit feedback.

**8.** Edit the presentation as necessary based on the feedback.

One of the benefits of breaking a task that you fear down in this manner is it can provide you with some insight as to what, specifically, about the task causes you to be fearful.

For today's lesson, take a moment to break down a task that seems difficult or almost impossible to you. This can be drafting a budget, preparing a speech, or even something as simple as planning a meeting that might help your employees understand your goals.

## DAY 2

> *"If you aim at nothing, you will hit it every time."*
> —Zig Ziglar, Writer

### Talk Time (to Yourself)

One of the most challenging things to do in life is learn how to talk to yourself. Negative thinking completely saps our motivation, and it ultimately comes from allowing fear to guide your thinking. We let fear essentially run our lives. Once you've recognized this cycle, you can and must change it.

Write down some negative thoughts in your life, regardless if they align with your actual fears. Make sure that you write down at least 10. Then think about what has made you feel that way.

## DAY 3

> *My failures are assets! I have laid the foundation*
> *for my life and today I am going to live that life!*

### I Think I Can, I Think I Can

"I just can't do it." Do you remember thinking that when you were in elementary school? You were learning so many new things then that you would take with you for the rest of your life, but you would often hear these words in the back of your mind when facing a new challenge. "I just cannot do it." It was so much easier to give up than to fail . . . but this was the fear of failure.

What things are you telling yourself in your personal or business life that you "just can't do"? Write them down today. Look at them. Then I want you to ask yourself, "Are these things really impossible?" Nothing is impossible!

Now write down something small you may be able to do to come closer to doing all those things that you keep telling yourself you can't! Think baby steps here. For example, if you want to climb Mount Everest, you'll need things like hiking equipment, travel arrangements, and skilled guides. Even if you're nowhere near ready for this journey, it is never too soon to take the first few steps and find ways to make your dreams possible.

## DAY 4

> *Failure is a stepping-stone. I will use my mistakes to learn, and I will not dwell on them. My mistakes will not steal my energy and focus.*

### Tick Tock, Try Again

It isn't worth my time. Do you remember a time in your life when you tried to do something new with your life? You could see yourself in a new job, or working on a new degree, but in the back of your mind you heard the voice, "It just isn't worth my time." Again, you let the fear of failure demotivate you. Trying and failing are only bumps in the road leading us to our full potential . . . right?

Think of something that you gave up a long time ago because it was too hard or took too much time. Could it have been part of your purpose? Is it something that is worth your time today? Get online and do some research. Can you still try it? Will it make you happy? If you still want to try, sign up today to participate in whatever it is that can lead you toward doing that thing again.

## DAY 5

> *What might have been is not a part of my vocabulary.*
> *I have tried, I have failed, and I have been successful.*
> *In any case, I am proud that I have tried.*

### Fighting Failure Over and Over Again

"I'll never do anything with my life." How many times have we thought this when we absolutely failed at something? It's so much easier to remind yourself of your failures than to keep trying. It's so easy just to give up. Remember, though, everything that we attempt to do in life is a stepping-stone to bigger and better things. Always motivate yourself past the fear that is plaguing you from reaching your full potential.

That's why today is such a big step. Write down what you will do with your life today.

Place that note somewhere that it can stay for a long time—on your refrigerator or your computer screen. Remember what you *can* do if you let go of negative self-talk.

## DAY 6

> *If my dreams are greater than my skills, then*
> *I am going to change my skills to reach my*
> *dreams. I will learn something new today!*

### Conquest and Conquer!

Today, think of another fear that you have that is stopping you from reaching your goals. Now, this might be a little tough, but I want you to conquer it today. Speak in public, even if it's only a few words. Grab that

15

business loan application that you are afraid might get turned down. Apply for that job you thought you would never get. Whatever it is, do it and write down how you felt afterward.

## DAY 7

> *My fears are my motivators. I need to defeat my fears if I want to be successful. I will defeat those fears.*

### Slicing Up Scary

Did you do something yesterday that scared you? Remember whatever the fear is, by breaking it down into more manageable chunks, you'll be able to spread those chunks out and climb over them more easily. And if even the chunks seem overwhelming, just continue to break them down into smaller bits to make them even more manageable.

Remember, you're ultimately in control, and there's great power in that knowledge.

Each time you face a fear and overcome it, no matter how small, you gain great strength. So do it continually. That strength turns into courage and confidence in what you are doing—no matter what form of "doing" you might be called upon to do. Write down in your notebook today, "The next time that I am up against [insert your fear here], I will [insert your strength]!" By facing your fears you gain the confidence to achieve your full potential.

## WEEK 4

# *Mentor Mentality*

I wonder how many mistakes I could have avoided by having someone to ask for advice. Now that you are learning to find your motivation toward goals and conquer your fears, it's time that you get a little help. It's hard to ask sometimes, but you can't do it alone. Whether you are transforming your business or are just a budding entrepreneur, the advice of someone who has been through it is worth millions.

## DAY 1

> *Relationships are important to my success. I will spend time today working on at least one of my relationships. I will find a mentor and follow the advice of those who care about me.*

### Your Question Quest

I was talking to a young entrepreneur yesterday whom I mentor, and it got me thinking about when I started my first business and how valuable it would have been to have someone to ask questions. There are all sorts of mentors out there—your friends and family, casual acquaintances, and even resources on the Internet. But only a true mentor can share the proper wisdom with you about how to successfully run a business.

Think of a few people you might consider to be good mentors. Write their names down and try to decide on the two best candidates for today.

## DAY 2

> *I can help others. I am a mentor. My*
> *thoughts and dreams will help someone, and*
> *I will share who I am with the world.*

### Moments with a Mentor

A mentor is someone with more business experience than you who serves as a trusted confidant over an extended period of time. Why would someone do this?

First and foremost, it is a way of giving back to the community while getting in practice as a teacher and advisor. Mentoring works two ways though, and the student often helps the teacher brainstorm ideas as well. So everyone wins.

Today, your task is to find the information that you need to contact a mentor. It's a big step to ask for help, but it will certainly be worth it. If you don't complete this task today, then hold yourself accountable and make it a top priority for tomorrow.

## DAY 3

> *I can deal with the best. I am one of the best!*
> *My life is important, and I will find others*
> *who believe in life the way that I do.*

### Listen and Learn

Mentors have the advantage of having learned from other people's successes and mistakes, giving them a "Been there, done that" type of firsthand knowledge. And honestly, it doesn't matter if your mentor has experience within your industry or understands the latest trends in technology. That's not why they are mentoring you—their job is solely to teach you about business and help you learn from their experiences.

Today is the day. Give your possible mentors a call. Ask them to meet and explain that you simply want some advice. Try to nail down actual dates and times as well, whether it's a meeting, a luncheon, or a follow-up phone call. Let's look at a couple of examples.

*Hi, Mr. Jones. I was wondering if you might have an open date when we could get lunch and talk about your career path and how you became successful. I'd also like to ask you a few questions about what direction I might take my career path.*

*Ms. Lewis, I have been a big fan of your work for a long time. I'm interested in learning more about how I can follow a similar career path. Would you be interested in meeting me for coffee one morning?*

## DAY 4

> *There are people in the world who want to help me and not only themselves. I am worth spending time with and my time is valuable.*

### Sometimes You Have to Search

Having a mentor is usually free, while a good coach or a consultant usually has a price tag attached. If you happen to be on a tight budget, then this is a major factor even though consultants will likely have additional knowledge about your industry. Organizations such as SCORE (Service Corps of Retired Executives) can help you find industry-specific mentors free of charge. Remember to show your appreciation by at least taking your mentor to lunch or doing something nice for him or her.

Today, come up with some questions to ask your mentor and write them down. Think about why you want to ask these questions and make sure you use them to gain as much information as possible.

## DAY 5

> *Great people help great people! I will focus on helping others today.*

## Expand and Assist

Expand your social network. Your mentor is an experienced business-person and likely has an extensive network. Your mentor is far more likely to assist you with making these contacts, and it places actual deci-sion makers within reach for your business.

Do some research into the connections your chosen mentor has. You can do this by exploring social media sites like LinkedIn and Face-book, or even researching the company your mentor works for. Spend at least 30 minutes today thinking about the introductions and connec-tions that you can ask your mentor about.

## DAY 6

> *I am a mentor! My strengths are weapons that can be used to teach others to defend themselves. I will be a mentor to everyone who crosses my path.*

## You Get What You Give

Your mentor should have no ulterior motive than to help you, and this will likely lead to a long-term relationship. As time passes and your friendship grows stronger, you'll also begin to see opportunities where you will be able to help your mentor as well.

Think about your future today and spend some time meditating on how you may be able to help your mentor. Think about what you and your business can become thanks to the help of your mentor. Write down one declaration of what you will do that could help your mentor one day.

## DAY 7

> *Investing in people is not easy, but it is worth it! I will face people with confidence and without fear of being hurt by them. I will invest in myself and others on a daily basis.*

*Remember and Rethink*

As you can see, having a mentor offers benefits and very high rewards with virtually no risk at all. The moments that you have with your mentor are a precious beginning to developing yourself as a respected and powerful businessperson. Use those moments to gain the knowledge that can help you succeed in all of your endeavors.

Today's assignment is simple: double-check the notes that you have taken along the way and make sure that you've written down exactly everything that you want to remember about your mentor and what he or she has told you. Then spend a little time thinking about the advice you've been given and how it can apply to your business today.

# *The Emotional Entrepreneur*

It's not always easy to start from scratch. Not only is it tough on most people financially, but it can weigh heavily on the mind that rests behind the idea. It's not always easy to keep your cool when the pressure is on and you are putting all of your ideas on the line. Maintaining a positive outlook, good energy, and a calm and cool demeanor will help you through this process. While it won't always be easy, I promise that keeping your emotions in check will help you to find success on your journey.

## DAY 1

> *I will try to focus my energy today and avoid the typical distractions that I face like workplace gossip, social media, and daydreaming. Today is all about focus!*

### Challenge: Mental Madness

No doubt, entrepreneurship requires significant mental energy. With its highs and lows, excitement and fear—which you may feel all at once—there are times when life feels too short and failure seems to be lurking close by. These feelings might not be fun, but they're normal.

After all, choosing entrepreneurship means you are choosing risk and acknowledging that the chance for failure is alive and well.

Now, write down what you are afraid of when it comes to business. Why are you afraid?

## DAY 2

> *Today I will not be defined by others' opinions of me! I will define myself and be true to who I am.*

### Challenge: Defining Yourself

When you get a job, your employer has a job description that describes what you need to do. When you become an entrepreneur, however, you have to decide for yourself the person you want to be. Why are you starting this business? What are your primary responsibilities? These questions can cause a lot of pressure.

Take some time to write down the answers to these questions. Think about how they make you feel and let go of the pressure.

## DAY 3

> *I will be independent. While I have learned that relying on others for help is necessary, I will make independent decisions that affect me and my company without the input of someone else's opinion. I am confident in my decision-making skills!*

### Challenge: Operating Under Little Guidance

Becoming an entrepreneur means starting with a totally blank slate—the business begins and ends with you. While that can sound pretty awesome, it also means you have little guidance—you have to create the map, including the destination and the directions to get there. It's easy for doubt to creep in. Be confident in your decisions and be okay with operating alone and carrying the weight of those decisions.

Write down a few decisions that you've recently made. Be proud of them. Display them somewhere that will remind you daily of those great decisions, no matter what the outcome was.

## DAY 4

> *The simple things in life are wonderful. I will take a moment today to reflect on all of the simple blessings that I receive on a daily basis.*

### Challenge: Embracing Your Emotions

Here's a question: What do you do when several intense feelings hit you all at once?

Doubt, passion, confusion, and fear are common—inside and outside entrepreneurship. But those emotions happen all at once—at great intensity—for entrepreneurs. With the lack of guidance and the stress that come with running a business, it's next to impossible to avoid these feelings.

Learn to embrace your feelings and use them to your advantage. Like an artist, express your business-self and break free from anything that might be holding you back. Make an artistic drawing again! This time use the words to describe what it is that you are breaking free from.

## DAY 5

> *When I start to feel anxious, I will find a way to calm down. If I need to step away for a moment, I will step away. It is better to have a moment away versus a day of stress.*

### Challenge: Stress Management

Never kid yourself into thinking that entrepreneurship is easy. The pressure can be overwhelming and until you learn how to manage and control the resulting anxiety, you just have to prepare for the gut-wrenching feelings coming your way in the early stages. Say your phone rings on the weekend or after hours. It probably means trouble, but you can't ignore it—nausea or not. You're in charge! So take a breath, answer the call, and deal with the situation.

Try a deep-breathing technique today. Breathe out for 10 seconds and then breathe in for 20 seconds. As you reach 20 seconds, hold your breath for 5 seconds. Do this as many times as possible today. Write down whether you think this exercise helped you. Take notes!

## DAY 6

> *My finances are just as important as my vision. I will make sure that I am in control of those finances and I will be resilient in caring for them.*

### Challenge: Financial Strain

When events go south, the first thing affected is always cash flow, the lifeblood of any company. And when finances are stretched to their breaking point, when that flow is cut off, you and your company are in big trouble. The subsequent chain reaction can be devastating to everyone involved in the venture, including your family.

Why then, if entrepreneurship is challenging in so many ways, do people keep becoming entrepreneurs? Easy. It's passion. With passion, we aren't boggled down by fear and self-doubt. It's a powerful feeling that reveals our greater purpose in life.

Write down one area where you may feel strained financially. Is there anything that you can do to fix it? Where can you cut back?

## DAY 7

> *I know that there are days that I will get overwhelmed. I am in charge of my sanity, and when those days come I will breathe, smile, and move on, remembering that if I am overwhelmed, then that means things are happening. Being overwhelmed is better than being underwhelmed. I will embrace overwhelmed!*

## Challenge: Reach Your Goals

If you find yourself overwhelmed by the psychological challenges of entrepreneurship, remember that they're all part of the journey—the destination you wanted and needed to go on. Building something out of nothing is not simple, which is why it's commendable that you've chosen this path. It'll get better, the challenges growing less intimidating and more controllable, if you just keep going.

Name one psychological challenge that you feel you face daily. Now place your goal on top of it! Write both down and envision that psychological challenge being destroyed by you achieving that goal.

# Success Strategies

Why do some people seem to be naturally successful? It's not that they don't experience setbacks, but when they do, they seem to recover smoothly. What's their secret? This week we are going to discuss exactly what to do when you think you've hit a brick wall. In some cases, your setback may be minor. In other cases, it may be something that is going to take a while to fix. In either situation, you must understand that it is only a setback and it does not translate to failure. It's just a hiccup, and eventually you can move past it and forget that you ever thought you might crash and burn.

## DAY 1

> *My behavior directly affects my success. I will behave as though I am successful, and therefore, I will be successful!*

### Adapt and Move On

Successful people actually develop behaviors that keep them at the top of their games. While they may face devastating situations, they understand that it doesn't mean they have to give up or start over. What they do is adapt. They realize that in order to make things work within their current situation, they must make a few changes. Sometimes changing is difficult and it's definitely not easy, but if you learn to adapt when you are in difficult situations, you are more likely to become successful in the long run. Because of the way adaptive people respond to situations—the same kinds we all encounter—they are able to continue to move ahead.

What situations might you need to be more adaptable in? Think about a time where you did adapt and it created success. Make a note of it in today's journal. Don't discount even the smallest of adaptations that you might have made. Be proud of every moment that you have seen a situation, changed your original idea, and been successful because of that change.

## DAY 2

> *I will remember to continue to learn. It is my goal today to learn one new thing, whether it directly affects my goals or vision, or if it does not. I will use what I have learned to grow.*

### Never Stop Learning

Successful people are always learning. With technology and trends constantly changing, new skills and perspectives are necessary. Successful entrepreneurs never say, "That's the way we've always done it." Instead, they seek ideas to do things in new and better ways . . . and they acquire the knowledge to make it happen.

Where do you need a new perspective? Spend some time today trying to gain a new perspective on something that you may be closedminded about. Write down what you can do to change your perspective.

## DAY 3

> *While my business goals are important to me, I will remember to set personal goals as well. Those goals are just as important as my business goals! I will focus on both sets of goals.*

## Establish Clear Goals

Successful people establish clear goals. Numerous academic studies have shown that people achieve more when given specific goals, rather than being encouraged to "do your best." People become motivated and achieve more when they know exactly what is expected.

Have you checked on your goals lately? Do you need to remind yourself? Write those goals down again! Maybe you've come up with another goal that wasn't originally on your list. That's okay! Add it in!

## DAY 4

> *Even when I feel challenged, I will do what is right and make the most of my time. Though shortcuts may seem appealing, I will focus on consistency and hard work.*

## Time and Time Again

Successful people manage their time well. Time management is a challenge for everyone, but entrepreneurs must become especially adept at making the most of their hours. Successful people are efficient. They prioritize their days, delegate whenever possible, limit time on nonessential tasks, and continually honor their schedules. You can do this by keeping a calendar close by at all times. Make notes of what you have going on and set up more than one reminder for important deadlines. A great way to do this is to get a dry-erase board calendar and five different colors of markers. Anything written in red is a high priority. Green can be medium priority, and so on. This way, when you look at your day, you know what needs to be done first and you associate each color with the deadlines you are facing. This tells your brain to do it *now*!

What nonessential tasks can you eliminate in your day-to-day life? Be as specific as possible. Think of tasks that can be done if you have extra time and write them in yellow. They are "maybes." By doing this, you will be excited when you've prioritized and can squeeze in a couple of "maybes."

## DAY 5

> *I will maintain a positive self-image. I am
> strong and successful, and I have something
> wonderful to share with the world.*

### Positive People Are Successful

Successful people have positive attitudes—and it's not that successful people expect every day to be totally happy. It's that they approach challenges with confidence and the expectation that most things can be worked out. Even a failure can provide lessons and wisdom that will be useful in the future.

In what areas can your attitude use an adjustment? When can you be a "Debbie downer" and what can you do to change it? Be brutal!

## DAY 6

> *Every person is important. I will remember to
> thank everyone I interact with for being a part of
> my journey. My network is my support, and I will
> respect those who are a part of that network.*

### You Need Support!

Successful people create a supportive network. Trusted friends and colleagues are part of every successful person's life. From lifelong childhood friends to a group of fellow inventors, people who can respectfully provide feedback and fresh perspectives (or just listen and help keep drama and worry to a minimum). A successful person's network also includes people who are simply enjoyable to be around—for lunch, fishing, or a drink after work.

Who is in your network? If you don't have a network, then today is the day to start establishing one. Write down one place that you will start looking and then . . . start looking. Social media is a great place to start networking. From there, you can find groups on websites like

LinkedIn where you can connect with entrepreneurs with similar interests to yours. Search message boards in your current city for entrepreneurs who are looking to connect. Can't find one? Post a message of your own and find like-minded entrepreneurs to connect with!

## DAY 7

> *Even when the day is dark and troubles are overwhelming, I will continue on with a positive attitude. I may not always be as successful as I'd like to be, but I will always have the opportunity to try again tomorrow.*

### Risky Business

Successful people take calculated risks . . . but the keyword there is "calculated."

Successful people know they must take chances in order to stay ahead of the competition. However, they perform analysis, consider the scenarios, and calculate the possible losses before they act. Risk is necessary, but not foolish.

What happens if they make a mistake? They dust themselves off and start anew.

It's exciting to be an entrepreneur! By watching others, learning from them, and then adding your own unique experiences to your strategy, you are on your way to becoming someone else's mentor and example. Name one entrepreneur you'd like to emulate and describe why.

# Manage Your Minutes

Your dream has always been to be your own boss, and now you've made that dream come true. Being your own boss allows you to do business the way you know it should be done—to offer a great product or service and to stand behind your promise. You've always known that you were going to make a difference in the world.

## DAY 1

> *My goals are important. My time is important. I will*
> *manage my time in order to achieve my goals today.*

### Time and Time Again

Time management is one of the biggest challenges you will face as an entrepreneur. You may have no resources other than yourself and your idea, so it seems logical that you have to keep working harder and harder. You're excited about your future, yet you're already exhausted.

Make a list today of what makes you feel like you don't have enough time. Are there particular situations that make things worse, or do you always feel like you need another hour?

## DAY 2

> *When I have time alone, especially at the
> beginning of my day, I will focus on me! I will
> concentrate on who I am spiritually today.*

### Slow Down

Everything needs to be done, all at once. How can you be sure you are making progress? Take a step back. Look at your list that you made yesterday and let's add to it. Ask yourself what you think can be done to help these time management issues. Make note of it so that you can compare as we go through each day this week and answer some questions.

Now it's time to make another list . . . but this is a good one. What would you do with an extra hour each day? How would you spend it?

## DAY 3

> *Today will be a day to complete short-term projects and
> make plans for long-term projects. I will focus on my goals.*

### What's the Plan?

Do I have a master plan?

This is a crucial question. Where do you want to be in one year, three years, or five years? Write it all down, regardless of how far-fetched or impossible it may seem today. It is only impossible if you can't set your sights on it to begin with; remember that anything is possible.

Start by making a list of your goals for each year. Be specific. How will you gain new business? How will you pay for things? Then break these goals down by month, and then by each individual week. Now you have a concrete plan to make progress. Each day, look at the week's list and get busy on the tasks.

## DAY 4

> *Problem-solving will happen today. From small issues to large problems, I will find a way to stay positive as I solve them one at a time.*

### Today or Tomorrow?

How will I spend today?

You know what needs to be done today, and how it will move you forward. Assign times to each task on your list to keep you on track. For example, spending four hours on a short blog post because you got sidetracked is not useful. Give that blog post an hour maximum and get it done. Also assign times for lunch, exercise, and occasional interruptions. Just know how your day is budgeted.

Stick to it! Write down exactly what your schedule should be like.

## DAY 5

> *I will find my desire and put that power into every task I face, no matter how menial it may be.*

### Be Wise; Don't Waste!

Does this task pertain to my goal?

As you consider your time, it's important to use it wisely. I suggest that at least half of your time should be spent engaged in activities that produce most of your results.

Make a list of the activities that you spend time on daily that do not produce results. Then decide how you can use the steps that you have learned so far to avoid wasting time on those activities. Make a commitment to cut out those time-wasting activities!

Then take your list of activities and write them on the schedule that you made yesterday. How much of your original schedule of things you really need to do can you still see?

## DAY 6

> *Today will be a great day. Staying*
> *positive is the key. I am successful!*

### Ditch the Distractions

Am I avoiding distractions?

Stay off social media while you work. Tell your family that your home office is off-bounds. Don't check e-mail every hour. Only take business calls during your scheduled work time. The easiest way to lose control of your day is to let time get nibbled away by distractions. When you discipline yourself, you'll have better focus.

Spend time today actively avoiding your biggest distractions. Do this each day until it becomes a habit. Write down how you felt when you did avoid certain distractions. What were they? Are there more?

## DAY 7

> *Somehow I will find a way to be creative*
> *today. I will do something out of the box.*

### Your Progress Is Precious

Is this the best use of my time?

As the company owner and leader, you want to have oversight of everything. In the beginning, it's how you measure your progress. But your time is precious, so ask yourself if your activity is in the best interest of success. Do you need to be putting stamps on mailings? Writing every blog post? Making a spreadsheet of contacts?

As soon as you can determine what to delegate, you give yourself the gift of time—time that can be spent growing your business. Write down your number one activity on a full page. Fold the corner of the page down so that you can go back and look at it any time that you might get distracted.

The hard work will never go away. And because you love your business, that's good news. When you learn to manage your time, you can do what you do best: become more successful!

# The Overjoyed Office

As a business owner, you know that you want to attract great employees. Whether you are just starting out and are hiring employees, or you already have a team in place, you know you want people to stay long term because job retention translates into profits when employees are knowledgeable and love what they do. The result? Fabulous customer service and job satisfaction.

Did you know that 70 percent of the people in the workforce are unhappy in their jobs?*

Regardless of any other factor (money, work schedules, benefits, etc.), 29 percent of employees will quit their jobs to find happiness.† On the other hand, 71 percent of today's workforce will stay in a position where they are bored, unhappy, and unenthusiastic.‡ As long as they collect that paycheck, they will stick around forever.

Think about your team—or your dream team you plan to have one day. Do you have some employees that fit these criteria?

---

* http://national.deseretnews.com/article/6427/most-americans-are-unhappy-at-work-heres -how-to-change-that.html
† http://www.usatoday.com/story/money/personalfinance/2014/06/29/retirement-life -reimagined-usa-today-survey/11135523
‡ http://www.gallup.com/services/178514/state-american-workplace.aspx, http:// www.forbes.com/sites/carminegallo/2011/11/11/your-emotionally-disconnected -employees/#80351a6e89b8

## DAY 1

> *While my goals are distant, there are things*
> *that need my attention today. I will focus on the*
> *tasks at hand today and not be distracted.*

### How Much Do You Care?

Here's an important question all entrepreneurs should ask themselves: "What makes someone really care about his or her job?"

This week we will go over those things and begin to create an office that is full of happy, caring employees.

Let's start with one of the biggest things: fair pay. Employees understand that all jobs are not created equal. The receptionist doesn't expect to earn the same as the chief financial officer. But when responsibilities are similar, people expect to be paid the same.

Can you think of a specific time that you felt undervalued because of your pay? Write about it!

## DAY 2

> *Today I will do something to make someone else*
> *smile. I will pay it forward and embrace humanity*
> *with kindness. Today I will be kindness.*

### It Only Takes a Little to Go a Long Way

Recognition. Everyone plays a part in a company's success. "Small" contributions can add up, making the workplace a great place to be. Taking a minute to acknowledge someone, writing a thank-you note, or starting a Rubber Chicken Award can mean more than you know. Never hesitate to give credit to those who deserve it.

Recognize at least one employee today for something that you normally wouldn't. Even if you are just starting with public praise, it is a step in the right direction. Take some notes about how you felt after you completed this random act of kindness.

## DAY 3

> *I will be thankful today, and I will tell my employees and coworkers that I am thankful for them. I am very blessed.*

### The Power of Praise

Feedback is another area of concern for employees. Closely tied to recognition, employees don't want to wait until their annual reviews to learn how they are doing. Honest and thoughtful feedback helps people know where to improve. Positive feedback motivates people to do even more.

Then again, what about all that petty stuff? We've all been there: a crisis or urgent matter causes us to dig in and make things better. But the little stuff that occurs in the office . . . all those dirty little things that drive us crazy . . . those things sap morale and divide our workforce.

Eliminate or minimize as many daily irritations as possible, and your staff will genuinely respect you for bringing the office together. So today, write down one way that you can remove an irritation from your workplace. You don't have to actually remove it yet, but make sure you've written down the idea.

## DAY 4

> *Today is a day to prepare for the unpredictable!*
> *When it happens, I will remain calm, knowing*
> *that I am ready for whatever I may face.*

### Remember to Relax

Control. The more employees feel they can take charge of their days, the happier they are. If you've hired well, then you have to trust people to do their jobs. Your door is open if they hit a snag or want your input but otherwise, expect that they will deliver on time, every time.

Try to take a step back today and relax. Maybe even leave the office for a little while. Let go today and see just what your employees have to offer. While you are gone, have them fill out an employee survey that asks for their feedback. Include a question about that "petty crap" and find out what might be going on that you don't know about.

## DAY 5

> *New ideas must be found, and I will constantly search for the next best thing, knowing that I must be an innovator. I am an innovator.*

### Change Is Good

Variety. It can be challenging to come up with new things for people to do, but everyone will appreciate a new challenge and the opportunity to tackle it. Boredom leads to disengagement, a company's worst enemy. Ask employees what they'd like to do or learn. You may be thrilled with the results.

Ask at least two members of your team what they'd like to see more variety in and come up with a way to implement that idea for a short amount of time today.

Then, write down whether this exercise was successful. How could it be more successful in the future?

## DAY 6

> *Without happy coworkers and employees, I will not be successful. I will focus on my company culture today, a culture of happiness.*

### Culture Is Critical

The happiest employees get along with their coworkers and spend time with them outside the workplace. An environment with flexibility, an attitude of acceptance, and supportive supervisors make people glad to come to work every day.

Leaders drive your company culture. When employees can respect and trust the leadership team, they feel secure. Leaders who are accessible, can communicate well, give honest reports, and listen to employees are key to job satisfaction.

Take a moment to analyze that survey you handed out and figure out what might be stressing your employees out. Brainstorm something that can help relieve that stress and implement it. Make sure to note in your journal how this changes morale in your office.

## DAY 7

*It's time to climb mountains by balancing my risks and rewards. Today I will climb. It may be risky, but my reward will be great. No FEAR!*

### Simple Rewards

Rewards. A University of Arizona study showed that offering rewards made teams more cohesive, even when the members didn't all get along. Incentives need not be expensive; things like time off, gift cards, or a special parking space can be very successful motivators. Later, we will expand on some bright reward ideas that any entrepreneur can provide on a budget.

As a business owner, the best thing you can do for your employees is to provide them with job satisfaction. When they are happy, they will do anything to make the company successful. In the end, everyone wins.

How did your employees react when you implemented a new change? How did you feel about it? Write a few words in your journal as you reflect on the week.

# Leadership Lessons

No matter what your business does, it takes more than one person to make it successful. Great businesses thrive because of outstanding teamwork. It's easy to bring a group of people together, but creating a cooperative and cohesive team requires the leader (you!) to help your staff be excited about working for a common goal.

## DAY 1

> *When I move forward, I am successful. I will take at least one step forward today.*

### Be a Leader

Lead by example. Don't ask your team to do something that you aren't willing to do. If you never stay late to finish a project, you can't expect others to give up their evenings.

Provide the tools. Do you know what your team needs in order to succeed? Ask them, and then listen. Really listen. Maybe they need different software or special training. Whatever it is, show that you're attentive and ready to support them.

Consciously try to begin providing tools for your team. Watch them work today. What is missing? What could help? Make sure that you write it down in your journal. Devote yourself to consistently keeping track of your progress.

## DAY 2

> *No more micromanaging! I will let other people*
> *help me today. I cannot do it all on my own.*

### Let It Go

Don't micromanage. If you picked the right people, you can let them run with their individual assignments. Checking on them causes team frustration and wastes your time. If you can't rely on others, maybe you need to re-evaluate your hiring process.

Another thing: be real. Leaders have emotions, too. When you can honestly share the joys and frustrations of a project, you're giving team members permission to be their authentic selves. Respect on both sides will grow and prosper.

Be real with at least two people today. Write down how it made you feel and what you think you can do better next time.

## DAY 3

> *I am a leader. Leadership is key to a successful*
> *product. I will be a leader today.*

### Mission Minded

Focus on the mission. Never lose sight of the reason your business exists. Teams certainly want to be involved in a profitable project, but as the leader, your job is to show employees how their work impacts the company's true purpose.

Take the time today to take note of exactly why your business exists. What was the mission that pushed you to be the leader that you are today? Write it down five times. Remember the words as you lead your team.

## DAY 4

> *Life is fun! I will find a way to have fun during my
> job today. Having fun will help me to be creative.*

### Laughter Is the Best Medicine

Have fun. Be sure to bring laughter to your team. Besides reducing stress and releasing endorphins, it creates a bond among team members. People look forward to working together when they can anticipate a positive experience.

Take time out of your day today to have fun with at least one member of your team. Whether it's telling a joke or organizing an office-wide dance break, do something out of the box and have fun with it. You know the drill: don't forget to write down how much fun you actually had.

## DAY 5

> *I know what I want and I will not stop
> until I get it. Today I will be relentless.*

### Have an Open Door and an Open Mind

Be available. You may not be involved in every project or committee, but you should be available for questions, comments, or requests as they arise. You'll also want to ask your own questions or get updates, so don't isolate yourself behind a closed door.

Leave your door open today, and swing the door of your mind even more wide open. Spend at least five minutes thinking outside of your box and ask your team to ask you questions that they may have been holding in. Write those questions down! Find the answers inside of yourself.

**DAY 6**

> *I am not perfect and no one expects me to be. When I mess up, I will stand tall, knowing that everyone makes mistakes and I must try harder to prevent myself from doing so.*

### Know Your Role

Admit your mistakes. Nobody's perfect, so when you flub something up, be a good role model. Likewise, admit when you don't know something. Transparency builds trust, and problems get solved faster.

Similarly, challenge your team. A healthy team welcomes the opportunity to create something or to solve a problem. A team that never leaves its comfort zone becomes bored. Encourage out-of-the-box thinking and challenge your staff to push you just as hard as you push them.

Run with an out-of-the-box idea today and see what happens. Make a note of it in your journal.

**DAY 7**

> *There is always room for growth. If I do not grow, those who look up to me will not grow. Today, I will continue to focus on moving forward.*

### Tend to Your Garden

Help your staff grow. Each team member has unique strengths and talents, and your business is going to need new leaders. People also become interested in new topics, which might lead to new products and services. Offer training and education in areas of interest.

When you treat your team members with honesty and respect, and prove your willingness to work alongside them, you will attract enthusiastic followers. People want to do a great job and have their efforts acknowledged. Start today and you can build a culture of co-operation.

Go out of your way today to try and get one unenthusiastic person excited today. How did that person react? How did you feel? Write those feelings down!

# Realistic Rewards

Your staff is terrific! Each one of them works hard to exceed goals and make the company a success. You want to let them know how much you appreciate all they do every day. Good for you! Employee recognition is the best way to keep people motivated and loyal.

## DAY 1

> *I'll find a way to give back today. Whether it is a simple smile or a substantial donation; I am going to find a way to make the world a better place. By doing so, others will be inspired by my actions.*

### Appreciate Your Team

In a landmark 10-year study involving more than 2.5 million employees around the world, only 51 percent felt appreciated.*

Take a moment to look over your employee recognition program (or your lack of one). Think about how you reward your team. Which of these rewards does your team strive for the most? Is it talked about often? If not, you may need to make some changes.

---

* http://www.eremedia.com/tlnt/weekly-wrap-employee-appreciation-its-not-as-good-as
-you-might-think/ http://www.gallup.com/poll/181289/majority-employees-not-engaged
-despite-gains-2014.aspx

Make a few notes of places where you may be able to add or take away from your current recognition program to make it more effective.

## DAY 2

*It's time to get organized! I will organize one area of my life today, small or large, and I will do it with a smile on my face. My smile will inspire my team!*

### Recognize and Reward

A study by *Forbes* stated that "83% of the organizations we studied suffer from a deficit in 'recognition.' And these companies are underperforming their peers."* Even on the tightest budget, you should recognize and reward great work.

For example, you can ask staff members to post recognition notes to each other on a bulletin board or internal website. Add testimonies from external customers. Then write down any reactions that you may notice from people who notice the notes.

Also, give people time off. Time is the most precious gift, and people will always remember that unexpected day off to do what they love. Go above and beyond and surprise an employee with a paid day off that is not taking away from their predetermined vacation days. Write down the reactions that you received after giving one hardworking employee unexpected time off. Did it help *you* in any way?

## DAY 3

*I am a force to be reckoned with! I will be a competitor and encourage my peers to do the same.*

* http://paybackincentives.com/the-secrets-of-employee-recognition

## Connecting and Caring Counts

A *Forbes* magazine report showed that 87 percent of employee recognition programs were based solely on tenure, not performance.* What do you base your recognition on and how do you reward it?

Do you want to really show a particular employee how much you care about him or her? Send a letter to the employee's family, telling them why their loved one is so important to the company's mission. Or here's another way—do one of the employee's least favorite tasks at work. Make sure that everyone gets the opportunity to see and understand that you are doing it specifically out of your appreciation for that worker. Then write about everyone's reaction in your journal.

## DAY 4

> *I enjoy being praised. Because of this, I will give others enjoyment by praising them today, and they, in turn, will reward me with their commitment and dedication to our company.*

## Innovative Ideas for Rewards

So, you are continuing to come up with new ways to reward your employees, but let's also make a list of some things that you might reward an employee for that are unexpected. Perhaps the employee has a clean desk or you notice the employee doing a job that might not be a requirement of his or her position.

Now, this won't work if it's an everyday reward that everyone is looking forward to, so it has to be something spontaneous to have the intended effect. For example, you could give an employee a cup of gourmet coffee or car wash gift card . . . just for going the extra mile.

Today's task should be fun. Give an unexpected reward to someone at work—it can be something practical (like a free lunch), enjoyable (like an iTunes gift card), or just downright strange and funny (like a

* http://www.forbes.com/sites/joshbersin/2012/06/13/new-research-unlocks-the-secret-of -employee-recognition/#1cfbfa9c2d94

rubber chicken or whoopee cushion). Just have a good time with it and write about the office's reaction when the gift was given. Then write about how it made you feel personally.

## DAY 5

> *I will find potential within myself and everyone I meet today. There is good all around me; I am going to be a part of moving forward with good!*

### Be Flexible

Science proves that recognition causes the brain to release oxytocin, the "love" hormone, and it makes people happier and more connected to their work. The result? Lower absenteeism, better workplace safety, and decreased staff turnover.

So here's today's task: plan a day to allow people to work from home or present them with a "flexible day" certificate. You'll be amazed at what gets accomplished!

Then consider giving departments their own week: Accounting Week, Programmer Week, and so on. Recognize the contributions made by these departments, take them to lunch, and make certificates to document their achievements.

## DAY 6

> *I am going to make sure that all of my employees feel valuable today. From the lowest level to the highest, I will recognize the sacrifices that they make for me.*

### Retaining Through Recognition

A 2012 Globoforce employee recognition survey found that companies with strategic recognition reported a 23.4 percent lower employee turnover rate compared to companies without any recognition program.*

That tells us that you need to create opportunities for your employees—become a mentor, chair committees, and do research on what opportunities your employees are seeking. Your company can also celebrate birthdays, weddings, graduations, and many other events that will bring people together for socializing and fun.

Find one reason to celebrate with your employees today. Then, write in your journal how productive they were after everyone got back to work.

## DAY 7

> *Today I will focus on effort instead of outcome.*
> *While all of my projects may not be complete,*
> *I will find happiness in the effort that has been*
> *put into each one by every person involved.*

### Effective Employee Engagement

According to the Aberdeen Group, "Being able to track the effectiveness of engagement and recognition efforts can help organizations better align engagement with business objectives and improve performance. 43% of Best-in-Class organizations have access to metrics on recognition efforts, compared to 18% of All Others."†

Establish a "Wall of Fame" for photos and clippings that recognize outstanding achievement. Mention your staff in the company newsletter and on your website as well.

Your goal for today is to write down three more fun ways to track employee recognition and announce at least one of them to your staff. Make it an open discussion and then once the method is decided, announce your first official recognition. Then write about how it made you feel.

---

* http://go.globoforce.com/rs/globoforce/images/SHRMFALL2012Survey_web.pdf
† http://www.globoforce.com/gfblog/2014/25-great-statistics-on-employee-recognition/

# Content Customers

With many choices in today's market, customers want to find brands they can love. When they feel valued and build trust with your company, they will truly love you. They will also become your best advocates for the life of your company.

> *Things may not always be clear to me, but I know that my vision will come to fruition. I will have faith in my vision, even when the outcome is cloudy.*

### Making the Connection

You have a fabulous product or service, and you are looking for customers who will love it as much as you do. The cool thing is that customers really are hunting for brands that they can love and keep buying, so it's just a matter of making the connection.

"People don't buy things for logical reasons," Zig Ziglar, world-renowned author and motivational speaker, once said. "They buy for emotional reasons." Can you think of a better reason to buy than *love*? Write down what you think you are doing to make customers love your brand.

## DAY 2

> *No matter how successful I become or how enormous my vision may be, I will remain humble in every aspect. Small steps will lead me to a magnificent outcome.*

### Know Your Customer

Know your "ideal" customer. Take a page from an advertisement copywriter and determine exactly who your best customers are going to be. Picture them: Where do they live? What kind of work do they do? What do they eat for lunch, and where do they like to vacation? How do they shop? How will your company serve them better than anyone else? The clearer the profile you develop, the easier it will be to find them and target your message.

Describe your ideal customer.

## DAY 3

> *When I am approached by change, I will embrace it! I will adapt to every situation, no matter how uncomfortable I may be with that change.*

### Practice What You Preach

Walk the walk, talk the talk. Use appropriate social media to reach out to your customers. In a January 2014 report by Pew Research Center, 71 percent of adults who went online used Facebook, but only 23 percent used Twitter.* Your lesson: show up where your customers are. Likewise, tailor your message's language and design to match your audience. You want to seem cool, not weird.

Think of that specific customer you wrote about yesterday. What can you do to tailor one part of your service to that customer? Write down a plan.

---

* http://www.pewinternet.org/fact-sheets/social-networking-fact-sheet/

## DAY 4

*I believe in my vision, and I will help others to believe in that vision with words of encouragement, professions of faith, and understanding that everyone within my company is vital and important.*

### Love Your Loyal Customers

Show your customers the love. You want customers to come back many times. So make them feel appreciated and always welcome the first-timer. Offer rewards and secret specials for those who are loyal. Woo back the ones who have gone away. When you make them feel special, customers will continue to choose you over a competitor. They just need reasons to stay.

Write down a customer reward plan today that you can reasonably implement. Make sure it is unique!

## DAY 5

*I will not be okay with okay! It's my passion to be innovative, and I will look for new ideas and new ways to grow and change as the industry grows and changes.*

### Be Creative Not Complacent

Keep the ways that you communicate and sell to your customers lively and don't let complacency set in. Introduce new products whenever possible. Have seasonal specials. Maintain your blog with interesting and timely topics. Use your website to track visitors, orders, and subscribers. With the proper software, you can also send offers that will be personal and enticing.

Research some software programs that could be useful to you. Are they affordable? What would you do differently that makes your rewards program stand out?

## DAY 6

> *My customers are my vitality. Today I will take time to be thankful for them, to show them appreciation. I will remember that I am not successful without a happy, loyal customer base.*

### Listen Up

Use active listening. Seek feedback from your customers, and then thank them. Comments—good and bad—are valuable. Talk directly with people, and make sure you spend time on the "front line" so you can observe customers' experiences. People appreciate when there is someone who can honestly listen and respond. When you are that person, they will love you for it.

Write down ways you can change your habits to be a better listener when it comes to the needs of your target market. Come up with one specific thing that you will implement.

## DAY 7

> *My vision is beautiful, but I will remember that I am not limited to that vision! I will keep my eyes open as opportunity may be hidden right around any corner.*

### If the Customer Isn't Happy, No One Is Happy

Stellar customer service. A Salesforce survey reported some compelling statistics: 73 percent of customers love a brand because of customer service. They also found that 70 percent of purchase experiences are evaluated based on how customers feel treated. In fact, 55 percent of customers say they would pay more for great customer service.*

* https://www.salesforce.com/blog/2013/10/customer-service-stats-55-of-consumers-would -pay-more-for-a-better-service-experience.html

Clearly, this is the backbone of your business. Hire well and never waiver from providing over-the-top customer service. What can you do to improve your customer service program? Are there things that need to be changed? Write down at least five ideas. Be critical of yourself!

# Voices of Victory and Execution

We all know that person who takes over the room as soon as he or she walks in. We all want to be that person, but many of us aren't sure how to execute the attitude! You are overflowing with great ideas, but somehow they don't ever seem to get past the idea stage. Sure, imagining things is fun. It's exciting to come up with fresh ideas, and it is a gift when you can do that. Following through, on the other hand, to execute those great ideas, is a learned skill.

I've asked several business leaders what helps them make people feel instantly comfortable and at ease and how they execute ideas and bring them to fruition. The answers you will read this week are many different strategies to win people over, and they are amazingly simple with some practice. Each day, practice their advice.

## DAY 1

> *I am confident in who I am. My smile is contagious, and I'm going to spread the joy I feel inside with everyone I meet!*

### Be Outgoing and Continue Journaling

Like I told you in earlier weeks, journaling is great for producing ideas. In addition to the notes that you are already making as you progress through this book, choose one word or a topic each day and write about it for 15 minutes. There's a second advantage to journaling. In addition to helping you produce ideas, it's a way for you to record ideas, and that's important. There's a time for thinking creatively, and for most people, that time comes in spurts. Enjoy it, because when things slow down, the work starts.

Practice smiling at everyone you see today, even if you feel weird. Say hello to strangers. Push yourself to the limit. Write down how you feel when you force yourself to smile.

## DAY 2

> *What I have to say matters. Even the smallest story might change someone's entire day. I will tell my story, and I will be honest, real, and genuine.*

### Have a Story and Narrow It Down

Thanks to your journaling, you have all those amazing ideas on paper. At least initially until you build better skills, choose one idea. Don't worry! You can come back to all those other great ideas once this one is successfully under way. You have them written down.

Tell at least one story to someone today. It can be the man next to you on the bus or your best friend. Practice telling great stories and they will come in handy someday when you are telling the story of your business or your product to a potential investor or to your customers. Write the story down in your journal so that you can use it again.

## DAY 3

> *My ideas are great, but humanity is greater. I will respect the gifts that humanity has given me and be compassionate throughout every moment of the day.*

### Be Compassionate, Create a Plan, and Designate Resources

No matter how big or small your idea, treat it with respect. Write a plan for executing it. Plans include a mission statement, sometimes a problem statement (something you want to fix), goals, objectives, and strategies. Larger plans have budgets or line up other resources required for plan execution. A mission statement is about your overall direction and purpose. You can use the same mission statement for a lot of different ideas. Objectives differ from goals in that objectives are measurable.

What resources do you need to make your idea real? Financial? Physical? Human? Part of planning is to figure out what you'll need and how you're going to get it.

Get in touch and appreciate the humanity in those around you. Being a kind, caring, and empathetic person will make others believe in you. Trustworthiness is a highly desired trait. Being narcissistic and cutthroat aren't.

Think of that part of human existence that you have compassion toward and do something about it today. Anything. It can be as simple as a hug or dropping a sandwich into a homeless person's guitar case. Do something today so that you can continue to grow; then note how it made you feel differently about who you are as an entrepreneur.

## DAY 4

> *There is no way for me to know who might end up being important in my world. I will approach people without judgment because that is how I would like to be approached. Today I will keep an open mind.*

### Be Nonjudgmental, Establish Marketing Points, and Create Measurements

Even though you display a strong sense of self, looking down on others is never a good way to work. There is a fine line between confidence and pretentiousness, and no one enjoys being judged based on looks, demeanor, or financial status. Your marking points along the path to completion are places in the plan or specific time points that you will pause to measure and evaluate.

You need a way to measure your objectives. You can measure with numbers, dollars, or progress toward execution, any type of measurement that is meaningful.

Spend some time thinking about someone you may have prejudged or overlooked. Try and see if there is another side to that person's story.

Make a journal entry of a person (or people) you may have prejudged unfairly. Then try to reach out to them today to see if they deserve a second chance to prove themselves to you.

## DAY 5

> *I will be consistent in doing what it takes to make my plan succeed. In addition, I will help and encourage others to succeed. I am a leader!*

### Be a Leader and Review Your Plan

In addition to measuring and evaluating at fixed points, review your plan every day. If you're starting off with a small idea you can complete in a day, review it whenever you get distracted. Your purpose in reviewing your plan is to make certain that you direct the activities in which you engage toward executing your idea. Is what you're doing contributing to or distracting you from your plan? This is the time to eliminate distractions!

Actively engaging others is instrumental in gaining people's respect and confidence. Don't be afraid to get your hands dirty, and lead by example. People are unimpressed with someone who just watches from the sidelines. Be an active cheerleader, rooting for the home team.

Are you a leader? Think about someone you consider a leader and what that person does that makes him or her a leader. We will learn later on exactly how to be a great leader, but for now, try to take small steps toward that goal.

Write down the name of one widely known person who you think is a great leader. Then read at least one article about what makes that person a leader. Also, take some notes about things within the article that inspire you.

## DAY 6

> *I'm going to face challenges. There will be tough times. Today, I will find a way to laugh through those times of change.*

### Be Humorous, Even Through Change

Being able to laugh at your own follies in the world at large can make others around you loosen up. Lighthearted people are literal magnets in the sense that others will want to be around you because you simply make them happy. Part of the process of evaluation is to realize when your strategies aren't working to accomplish your objectives. You might even realize that your idea isn't going to work. If that's the case, congratulate yourself that your plan allowed you to discover that before you wasted precious time, energy, and other resources trying to proceed with an idea that's unworkable!

Make someone laugh today. Even if it is a child. Laughter is oxygen for growth, both in your business and personal lives. How did that make you feel? Be honest!

## DAY 7

> *When things go well, I understand that it is okay to celebrate! Today, in the midst of an accomplishment, I will celebrate my success. It's a good thing to be happy!*

### Have Passion and Celebrate!

What are you truly passionate about? Is it the same as your purpose? Should it be? Take some time today to think about what you are passionate about . . . and then be passionate today. You can do this alone or out in the world. When your passion comes to fruition, it's natural to want to cheer a bit. Even a small project deserves a pat on the back from yourself for completing it. Every project deserves a time that you can sit back and look at what you've done and appreciate the real results of your work.

Some people go through these steps very naturally when they have an idea. They don't even notice that they're doing these things! But some of us need a little help, some training. Apply this exercise to carrying out a few of your ideas, and pretty soon you'll do it naturally too!

Just remember what it feels like to be on fire for something; write down what you did, why, and how you felt afterward.

# *Marketing ME*

You can be the best writer, lawn service technician, or anything else, but if no one knows you exist, what good is it? You do not have to be a professional salesperson to market yourself; you just have to believe that what you do will benefit others.

Some people know they are good at what they do, but they simply struggle to put it into words for others to hear. This week we will focus on that very problem.

## DAY 1

> *I will have faith in my intuition today. There is no need for me to chase down the market. I will trust my gut and let the market come to me.*

### The Difference Between Marketing and Advertising

There is a difference between marketing and advertising. While both components are important, they are very different. Knowing the difference can put you and your company on the path to substantial success.

Advertising is making customers aware of an individual product or service that you're selling. Some forms of advertising are flyers, newspapers, e-mails, radio, websites, magazines and more. Marketing is a much broader activity people and businesses do that is more involved. Some of the things marketing includes are researching, selling, advertising, and public relations. So the big question is: How do you market yourself by selling yourself? This week will teach you four ways to do that.

Write down what you think you are already doing to market yourself. Is it working? Why or why not?

## DAY 2

> *There are things that make me and my company special.*
> *I will focus on those things instead of the things where I feel*
> *like I am lacking. Everyone is different and that is okay.*

### Evaluate

Evaluate yourself. How are you different? What do you represent? Why should people be interested in what you have to offer? These answers are some of the most important aspects to marketing yourself. When you know these answers, you build confidence.

Make a list of at least five things that make you different. Think about how those things will help you achieve success in selling yourself.

## DAY 3

> *When a great idea comes to me, I will*
> *trust my gut. If I meet someone new and feel*
> *uneasy, I will trust my gut. I believe in my own*
> *intuition and will trust myself at all costs.*

### The "You" Pitch

Create your own 20-second pitch—or commercial—about why people should trust your business instincts.

Why just 20 seconds? In today's world, people are on the move. They want answers now and will only listen until the information is not important to them. So your 20-second commercial should only include the bullet points of who you are, what you have to offer, why they should choose you, and how your offer benefits them.

Write down a script for your commercial today. Be honest and concise. Use it as you prepare to sell yourself.

## DAY 4

> *Marketing myself is important, especially to those throughout the world. Today will be the day that I focus on my digital footprint. I will push to leave as large of a print as possible!*

### Social Media Rules

Do you have a great online presence? Do you have a LinkedIn page, an online resume, a professional website or a blog (including head shots), and possibly other social networking sites? Does your personal social media account reflect your image? Marketing yourself online is just as important as offline. You will be surprised at how well you will sell yourself online because people you want to be in front of will look through your online information.

Spend some time today updating your profiles. Make them as expressive as possible while maintaining the utmost professionalism.

## DAY 5

> *Relationships are important to my career and my business. I am important to other people's relationships. Today is a day to embrace who I am in each of those relationships and use that to better my world.*

### Relationships Matter

Build relationships. By building relationships, you build recognition. Those who know you best will talk about you to others, and this is another form of marketing yourself. You can also build relationships online by joining groups or forums and participating in them. Social networking is a two-way street, though, so you have to give as much as you take.

Marketing yourself is most effective when you have a good knowledge and understanding of yourself, your skills, and your abilities. Whether you have a business or are planning to go into business for yourself, certain skills can help you to market yourself by selling yourself first.

Write down the things about your business that you think make it a bestseller. Are you utilizing those things?

## DAY 6

> *I am motivated to change my world. Nothing can stop my motivation, and when I feel low, I will use that to push me even closer to my goal!*

### Motivation

Stay motivated. According to *Merriam-Webster*, motivation is a force or influence that causes someone to do something. The question is: What motivates you? If you work for someone else, is it pressure from a boss? If you're in business for yourself, is it pressure from a customer? Or are you one of those fortunate individuals who are self-motivated?

We will learn a lot of tools toward motivation later, but for now, try this trick: Take a blank sheet of paper and draw a large square on it. Then divide the square into four quadrants. In the upper left quadrant, write your ultimate goal (e.g., annual gross sales). In the upper right quadrant, write an interim benchmark (e.g., monthly gross sales). In the lower left quadrant, write another interim benchmark (e.g., how many presentations you'll need to make each week to meet the monthly benchmark). Finally, in the lower right quadrant, list the tasks you will need to complete today to achieve your weekly benchmark.

By breaking your ultimate goals down using the goals quadrant, you can actively monitor your goals on a daily basis. That daily monitoring will not only keep you on track toward achieving your goals, it will help keep you motivated every day.

## DAY 7

> *Change can be a good thing. I am good with change! In order to meet my goals, I must embrace everything that comes my way.*

### Adjustments Are Okay

As you monitor your goals, you will undoubtedly need to make adjustments in some of your daily tasks in order to keep you on track toward meeting your interim benchmarks and, in turn, your ultimate goal. That's to be expected.

The best time to review your goals and make necessary adjustments is first thing every morning. That may seem like a lot of work, but a daily review is essential to staying on track and staying motivated. To make the adjustment process easier (and less time consuming), I recommend creating your goals quadrant in electronic format so that changes can be made without having to rewrite the entire document.

Whether you adopt the goals quadrant method or choose another methodology that we will learn later, monitoring your goals daily is an easy way to get and keep yourself motivated. Write down which specific goals you are going to monitor and hold yourself accountable for.

## WEEK 14

# *Expect and Inspect*

Many individuals have a hard time finding the motivation to set the goals we talked about a few weeks ago. This is largely due to the very nature of goals—they are in and of themselves a form of delayed gratification. However, we've already learned some tricks about motivation, and now we can use them as we lay out our goals. Remember, goals are things we wish to achieve in the future. The common adage "don't expect what you don't inspect" can help you in finding the motivation to set goals that you will accomplish!

## DAY 1

> *It is my job to be realistic about every situation. I will keep my eyes and ears open in order to assure that I am fully aware of my situation at all times.*

### Don't Expect What You Don't Inspect

Don't expect what you don't inspect. This adage is applicable in both our personal and business lives. Let's start today by breaking this saying down into two parts.

The first things we see are the words, "don't expect." The act of expectation is really what we can think of as goal-setting. Expectations equal goals. When you think of it that way, are your expectations realistic? Do your expectations align with your goals or are they much different?

Spend some time today writing a sort of pros and cons list. First, write down your expectations for your business. Separately, write down your goals for your business specifically. Do they match up?

## DAY 2

> *In order to manage my stress, I have to maintain some control in my life. I will use that control to propel me toward my goals!*

### What Are Goals?

Goals are the objects of our ambition and effort. We set those goals to assure that our efforts are productive. The goals become expectations that we have for ourselves and our business. These expectations are vital in order to make sure we are moving in the right direction. You need to set your own personal goals that are separate from your business goals. Both aspects are vital to your success.

Think about what goals you have for yourself, separate from your business. Do you want to buy a house, a car, or something else? Are you saving for your children's college education? Do you want to run a marathon or climb a mountain? What goals do you have? What will it take to achieve them?

Have you set your personal goals to coincide with your business goals? If so, write down a couple of personal goals that are completely separate from your business goals. In fact, don't think about your business at all when you write them down. Spend time today meditating on exactly how you can achieve those goals for one person only: YOU.

## DAY 3

> *My goals are a measurement of my success. If I have not reached my goals, I will strive toward one specific goal today. Today I will reach at least one goal!*

### There Is Value in Your Goals

Goals can be used as valuable yardsticks in order to highlight success or judge failure. If you are not setting personal goals in business, then you are limiting your ability to leverage your successes to your superiors and stakeholders. From a management perspective, if you don't set goals for your team, the team will lack direction and guidance.

Yesterday you set some personal goals that don't relate to your business. Today set some personal goals that do relate to your business and compare the two. Make sure that you keep your focus in order to maintain your motivation. Make sure that you are setting realistic long-term goals. Think about that as you write in your journal this week.

## DAY 4

> *When I fail in the now, I will look toward my long-term goals and remember that with every step backward, I will find a way to leap forward.*

### Types of Goals

There are two types of goals. You need to set both short-term and long-term goals. First, I recommend setting your long-term goals. Do this by asking yourself: "What are the fundamentals that define success for my organization?" Some examples of these are profitability, sales, customers served, and so on.

It is important to accurately determine these critical aspects of your business before setting goals in order to ensure that you are incentivizing the correct behavior.

Yes, it's that time again. Write down some long-term goals that you will stick to. This time, write down what motivates you to complete those goals, both from your personal expectations and your business expectations.

## DAY 5

> *Today I will focus on managing each of my goals differently. I will not grow disappointed in those long-term goals that are not yet accomplished. Instead, I will relish in the small, short-term goals that are finite.*

### Short-Term Goals

On the other hand, short-term goals allow for faster gratification for your team. They also allow for faster correction if something isn't working out as you intended. If short-term goals are not being met, then the team needs to know in order to get the ship on the correct course. Furthermore, these short-term goals help build team cohesion and buy-in to the goal-setting process. Studies have shown that celebrating these small wins together will lead to more wins.

What are some simple short-term goals that you know you can accomplish? How will they help you reach your long-term goals?

## DAY 6

> *I will stop doing things that do not make me happy. If I am reaching for goals that do not lead to happiness, I will change those goals. I deserve to be happy!*

### Relax and Review

Now that we have briefly covered two types of goals, let's revisit our adage "Don't expect what you don't inspect." Since the goals are your expectations, it is time now to review inspection. This is one of the most important parts of your goal-setting process. In and of themselves, goals are useless if you don't inspect them.

How do you inspect something that hasn't been reached yet? Simple. Go back and look at the goals you've written down this week, both personal and business. Are you happy? Are you still motivated? Are you on track for sales? How do you look financially?

It's very important for you to inspect, to look deeply into these questions today as you write in your journal. You will have a harder question to answer tomorrow.

## DAY 7

> *I will focus on the positive. My past does not determine my future, and I refuse to allow it to dictate my today! I am getting closer to my goals every single day.*

### What Are You Doing Wrong?

If you are not reaching your goals, then what are you doing wrong? Is it because you've set an unattainable goal . . . or is it because your motivation has not been driving you like it should? In any case, we need to make sure that your goals are realistic.

In addition to looking into yourself for the answers to these questions, it may also be profitable to bring in someone with a fresh perspective. So, instead of writing anything down today and depending on yourself for your motivation, find a friend.

Ask someone for his or her opinion on your goals. Take that person's advice seriously and use it for your benefit. Remember, you need to surround yourself with people who encourage and inspire you. Be sure that you are keeping good company.

# The Professional Powerhouse

Let's take a step back from yourself this week and have a look at your employees, coworkers, customer base, and networks.

Have you noticed how successful people seem to easily expand their networks? Or how they are able to ask colleagues for assistance with just about anything? It may appear that they are more confident or sophisticated than others, but they actually are following a simple model of behavior that leads to lasting and loyal professional relationships.

## DAY 1

> *I know that I am complicated. I know others are complicated. I will choose to approach others as I would want them to approach me—with an open mind.*

### Levels of Success

Successful people are kind to others at all levels. It's not always easy smiling at the guy who seems to have all of the good stuff fall into his lap without working for it, but if you want to be successful you will learn to smile and breathe through any animosity that you may be feeling.

Having respect for your colleagues and employees in every position is not only the right thing to do, it's also a way to network. Acknowledge the responsibilities of every staff person; an organization's success depends on each team member. You never know exactly who is going to be able to help you along your road to success.

Think of one person who just gets under your skin and try to go out of your way to be nice to him or her today. Then reward yourself. Make a note of what your reward was.

## DAY 2

> *Today I will be useful to someone other than myself. There is honor in purpose and outside of my goals, my purpose is to help others.*

### Don't Hesitate!

Successful people don't wait to be asked for help. They offer it just because. Successful people will provide information when they hear that someone else needs it. They send links to articles, the name of a good plumber, and referrals to other colleagues. They find mentors for new staff members.

It's not always easy to give without receiving, but in the larger scheme of things, we must believe in some kind of karma. The old sayings, "what goes around comes around" or "what you reap is what you sow," are very applicable.

Spend some time giving today without receiving, and it will come back to you eventually. Write down what you did specifically.

## DAY 3

> *If things go wrong, I will embrace the fact that I*
> *tried and use the situation to learn something. I will*
> *be honest and upfront in all aspects of my life.*

### Own IT!

Own your behavior. Everyone makes mistakes. What's different about successful people? They don't wait to get caught; they are honest and upfront about their mistakes and decisions.

The fact of the matter is that you are going to mess up. You are going to have ideas that don't work out. Successful people stand up and take ownership for their mistakes just as quickly as they own up to something that worked out in their favor. Make sure that you are standing up for what you believe in every time you speak. Not everyone is going to love you for it, but you will love yourself, and that is the most important thing.

Today, write down 10 things that you believe in and that you want to stand up for no matter what.

## DAY 4

> *In order to be a champion, my team must succeed*
> *along with me. I will sacrifice for my team and*
> *work for them as much as I will for myself.*

### Successful People Know When to Take a Hit for the Team

A true leader will not pass blame to a colleague or staff person. It may seem so easy to just push the blame on to a person who is deserving of it. In fact, it is easy. But easy isn't always right, is it?

To be successful, you need to know when it is the right time to take one for the team. It's not going to be fun and your day may pretty much be ruined. However, if you step in to handle a demanding situation or angry customer instead of sitting back and letting someone else deal with it, you will gain respect from your coworkers.

Think about a situation where someone took one for you. How did you feel? What did it make you think of that person? Make a note! Don't forget.

## DAY 5

> *Today I will remember to see things from perspectives other than my own. My opinion is not necessarily the truth. I will listen to what others have to say.*

### Perspective Matters

Asking for someone's perspective says that you value the person's experience and intelligence. Even if you have already formulated your own opinion on a subject, it doesn't hurt to ask someone else for theirs. Doing this also means that you are willing to listen to people who may disagree with you. This is a great sign of a successful leader.

When you have the capability to listen to someone you know will offer an opinion that is not necessarily the same as yours, it provides you with an abundance of power. The other person may have valid reasons that you may not have considered, and it may actually help you in the long run.

Take a moment today to listen, really listen, to another person's perspective on a situation that you are dealing with. Make sure that you really consider everything that person is saying before deciding on your own opinion.

Then, write down two different scenarios of the situation so you can see things from both points of view.

## DAY 6

> *I want to help other people by introducing them to successful relationships and connections like the ones that I have. Today I will be sure to help at least one person connect with another.*

### Successful People Connect People

Successful people connect people. What does that mean?

Successful people are generous in their introductions and in helping people find needed resources. Even if the resource or connection does not relate directly to you, it could change another person's entire world. When you help other people connect and offer up an introduction or the opportunity to combine ideas, you are helping the greater good of your company, as well as those people.

One of the benefits of networking is to get to know a variety of people, and then to use your network to connect those people who might not know of each other. Eventually, those people will send connections back to you that will help with your own projects.

The next time a colleague needs a referral or even asks for one for a friend, offer it up. Write down a practice referral letter for someone that you have confidence in.

## DAY 7

> *There is something more to come each and every day. I know what I was born to do today, and I will do it. If tomorrow brings a different goal, I will reach for it with passion.*

### Successful People Are Genuinely Thoughtful and Considerate

They offer congratulations and acknowledge achievements. They send e-mails to maintain connections. They send gifts and remember important days. They are delighted when others succeed. These are just a few traits that can show thoughtfulness in the workplace. Sometimes it may seem like the smallest thing, but a genuine sense of consideration will get you a long way at work.

Real success is impossible without building and maintaining authentic relationships. When you treat others with respect, you will be rewarded both professionally and personally.

Make a note of three different ways that you can respect those that you work with and around unexpectedly.

# Serving Success

Whether it's tennis, volleyball, or even ping-pong, most sports require a serve and a response. In business, whether intentional or not, leaders serve and employees respond. And if leaders adopt a mindset of serving, then employees respond more positively and more productively.

This week, let's work out the seven muscles of your leadership skills and see how sweet we can make your swing.

So, let's put this swing into a business situation. A software glitch brings production to a screeching halt and now that crucial deadline appears as if it won't be met. Everyone has an opinion on a solution, but time is of the essence. Enter the inspirational leader! He or she brings sanity to the chaos and knows how to inspire staff and employees. So what does this person have that you don't?

## DAY 1

> My integrity will help others to trust me. I
> will live with integrity that does not falter,
> even when tempted. I am trustworthy.

### The Trust Tendon

According to an article in *Forbes*, leaders like the late Nelson Mandela had so much influence because people knew they could trust him. His word was his bond. The article from *Forbes* went the next step by explaining: "This same sentiment can be carried over into the workplace, where employees want their leaders to be more trustworthy and transparent. Employees have grown tired of unexpected outcomes resulting from the lack of preparation."*

If you want to inspire your team, keep your promises, big and small.

Make sure today that you carefully choose what you promise to your team. Think about your words and be sure not to make any suggestions or promises that have no possibility of coming to fruition. Don't fake the serve. Earn the trust of your team and they will be an asset. And it is only when we communicate our beliefs authentically that we can attract others to our cause, and form the bonds that will empower us to achieve truly great things.

Some managers and leaders want to withhold information from their employees. Often, it is done because of a lack of trust. No one wants to live in fear, especially when we are afraid of the people who hold the most sway over our professional lives. Trust isn't given overnight. It's developed by intentional leaders who find ways to include their employees, make the work environment safe, and entrust significant responsibility to them. It starts with a leader taking the time to train employees and allowing mistakes and the space to grow.

Write down two things that you think you can do to earn more trust throughout your business.

## DAY 2

> There will be days when I am tired, but I will maintain my enthusiasm. A good leader always behaves in the manner that the team should behave. I will be eager and bold, even when I may not feel that way on the inside.

### The Elbow of Enthusiasm
If you aren't enthusiastic, your team won't be. The keys to inspiration are intense and eager enjoyment, showing interest, and putting your

* http://www.forbes.com/sites/glennllopis/2013/12/09/7-reasons-employees-dont-trust-their-leaders/#2e1f2eb81a20

stamp of approval on ideas that excite you. There's no way you can serve the ball if your arm doesn't have the capability to bend.

Also, inspirational leaders rarely just take a walk, they walk with a purpose. The point is for you to have a plan and excel at sharing that plan. The most detailed vision won't do a bit of good if you can't enlist the help of your staff and employees. Be an excellent communicator.

Come up with a plan just for today. It doesn't need to go any further than today, just start small. If you aren't a planner, this may be difficult for you and you may need to write it down to hold yourself accountable. So write your plan down either way.

## DAY 3

> *Today I will be optimistic in the face of doubt. When darkness dares to cloud my vision, I will remember that my goals are near and there is nothing for me to fear!*

### The Acromioclavicular Air of Optimism

Also called the AC joint, the acromioclavicular joint allows you the ability to raise your arm above your head. It acts like a strut to help with movement of the scapula, resulting in a greater degree of arm rotation. If you hold on to your optimism as a leader, then the rest of your team can do their jobs without worry, just like the rest of the arm. Without rotation, your swing will be useless.

The workplace atmosphere plays a big role in how well your team performs. That being said, you can't pretend that problems don't happen. Encourage optimism. In fact, insist on it but don't run from troubleshooting. Great leaders face problems head-on and look for positive solutions.

Think of a way to inspire your team with optimism today and go for it! Did it work? Write one thing you could have done differently as well as their response to your optimism.

## DAY 4

> *People need to be aware of my presence. I have important things to say, and I will be sure to voice my opinion, even in awkward situations. I am a force for good!*

### The Invisible Inferior Radioulnar

Injuries to the inferior radioulnar joint at the wrist often result from falls on an outstretched hand. Injury can occur when the leading joint of the arm can be isolated. If you are outstretched, visible, and blaring when your team has a fall, everything behind you will be useless.

Watch a team sport and the players all basically look the same. Everyone has the same uniform and the same color. If you watch long enough, the true leaders emerge not because of a uniform, but because of an ethic.

The same is true in business; it's not the office or the title that makes the leader. It's the work ethic and the example a leader sets. You don't need to be recognized as the hand that is holding the racket that will ultimately decide on the outcome of your swing; you need to be invisible, one of the team, simply part of the arm.

True leaders aren't afraid to roll up their sleeves and get their hands dirty right along with the other members of the team. It's this modeling of desired behavior that will lead employees to follow suit.

Think of three leaders that you have respect for and write down their names. What traits do they have that you would like to emulate?

## DAY 5

> *I will exude power. It is not necessary for me to notify others of my presence and power. They will respect me more as a leader if they can feel and respect that power instead of being told to adhere to it.*

## The Pronate Power

Pronation at the forearm is a rotational movement where the hand and upper arm are turned inward. In a nutshell, traditional leadership is more about accumulation and exercise of power, while servant leadership is about growth and well-being of employees. Servant leadership is not having managers cater to their employees, but it is leading by example, they turn in toward the employees and understand what being a member of the team is like from their point of view.

Let me share a practical example. For years at my office, we had a designated parking area. Management decided to suggest that employees park in a new area farther from the door. It wasn't a mandate though and I really liked my old parking spot. But when I saw my boss park in the new area that was farther away . . . and he was lugging more gear than me, well I was moved—literally. I started parking in the farther lot as well. Mandate or not I followed the example set before me. It wasn't the power that moved me to act, but the action of those in power.

What can you do as a boss to inspire your employees to follow mandated rules? Think about it, write it down, and put it into action tomorrow.

## DAY 6

> *Other people look up to me and need my help. I*
> *will offer my services to anyone who needs a boost,*
> *especially if those services will help them reach*
> *a higher level in their field or career path.*

## The Supine Suck-Up

Supination of the forearm occurs when the forearms or palms are rotated outward. In the workplace, we want employees who are not boss-watchers or boss-pleasers. These types act one way when the boss is away and totally opposite when he or she is present. Those are not the types we need in our business though; we want an employee who looks outward and who looks out for the best interest of the company.

Servant leadership will build the type of community where employee and employer can work together toward a common goal no matter who is watching. Suck-ups suck, and not just figuratively. They drain the workplace of integrity. Morale goes out the window. Employees with character want to know that their leader can see through the deception of others. Lead at a higher level to cultivate an environment of mutual trust and respect.

How can you earn more respect from your employees? Make a list of five things and implement one for the next five days.

## DAY 7

> *My team will support me and I will support my team! We cannot succeed without one another and it is my job to lead my team toward that success.*

### The Fist to Follow

Are you a leader or a driver? People ask the difference between a leader and a boss. "The leader leads, and the boss drives" is a great quote from Theodore Roosevelt. The following differentiates nicely the difference between a servant leader and a traditional leader:

A boss drives employees, depends on authority, inspires fear, places blame, knows how it's done, takes credit, and flat-out uses people. A leader, on the other hand, coaches employees, depends on goodwill, generates enthusiasm, shows how it's done, and always gives credit when credit is due.

Which type of leader are you? The ball is in your court and it's your serve. Write down the type of leader that you are and then write down the one that you want to be. Make a list of things that you can do to become that particular leader.

# Take a Break

As I get older I am constantly reminded and much more aware of how much we need to depend on others. Our connections to others are the key to our survival, happiness, and success. So how do you make your interactions stronger? This is a challenge many entrepreneurs have, especially since we are all superbusy.

Sometimes, to make the most of our relationships, we actually need to spend some time alone. Not all of us are comfortable being alone, but it's important to acknowledge that discomfort and explore it because the benefits of alone time are important. In fact, alone time is the critical balance to social connection for our health and productivity. This week let's learn about ways to spend some time alone and how they will benefit you in the long run, ultimately making you more successful.

## DAY 1

> *Today I will take a step back and look at my goals.*
> *I will stop multitasking and focus on one project at a*
> *time until I see things from a different perspective.*

### Just Say "NO" to Multitasking

We now know that human beings are not natural multitaskers. Most of us move rapidly from task to task, reducing performance and effectiveness. And multitasking adds to stress. You probably don't think of responding to others as a "task," but in the sense that awareness of others requires attention and energy, it is. And if there are two people in the vicinity, being aware of and sensitive to each is like two "tasks." Removing that input for a period of time while you focus on one or two things reduces stress.

If being alone is difficult for you, it's important to explore why this is and practice being alone. If you are not comfortable being alone with yourself, relationships by definition will be codependencies. When you learn to enjoy your alone time, you can come to others as a full, not a needy, person.

Spend some time being aware today in a way that you might not have done in the past. Think before you spend time on a task and dwell on exactly how that can reduce the stress that you are feeling.

## DAY 2

> *My day will be better if I spend a few minutes*
> *of it alone and disconnected. I will look around,*
> *think, and be grateful for the things that I have.*

### It's All About Balance

It's important to balance alone time and social connection. All the world's religions recognize the importance of this balance and encourage private spirituality as well as community engagement. In today's world, fragmented as we are, we often don't do a very good job being alone or connecting. Despite our constant connectedness through social media, 50 percent of Americans are single (vs. 22 percent in 1950), and 27 million live alone (vs. 4 million in 1950).* But how well do we use that alone time? Learn to use it effectively, and your social connections will be more effective as well.

Make a point to spend at least 15 minutes alone today, disconnected completely. Take a walk, sit quietly, or take a bath, but do something alone, without a phone, the Internet, or the need to answer the door.

---

* http://www.pri.org/stories/2014–09–14/singles-now-outnumber-married-people-america -and-thats-good-thing

Fifteen minutes. Think about how you are going to try and quit multitasking for the rest of this week.

## DAY 3

> *Today I will be centered, intuitive, creative, and*
> *reflective. I will find opportunity within conflict.*

### Be Alone!

Studies show that you are more creative during alone time than when involved with others in brainstorming. When you spent that time alone yesterday, did you come up with any new ideas? Write them down today and then be very aware of what you were thinking. Now that you have less to focus on and you've quit multitasking for a while, you are more aware of yourself, your emotions and thoughts, and your surroundings.

So alone time is important for you to be your best possible self. It's easier to get this time than you think! Schedule alone time on a regular basis—at least once a week. Learn to close your door. Get up and get into your office early. Use your lunch break effectively. Take a walk by yourself. Look up at least once a day.

## DAY 4

> *Even amid distractions, I will not lose my focus*
> *and I will continue to reach for the prize. I have*
> *the ability to win, and I am on the right path!*

### Be Effective!

Now that you are not multitasking and you are spending some time alone, without distractions and have the ability to think, you can complete projects with greater satisfaction.

With fewer distractions, you will complete projects more effectively and with greater concentration and they will be more successful. Because you're not multitasking, completing the project will bring you greater satisfaction and will serve to reduce stress instead of increase it. Think of one project that you've been trying to complete for a long time. Focus on that project and don't let anything get in the way until you've finished! No multitasking on this one. Just complete the one specific project and do it alone if you have to in order to get it done.

> *I will nurture my mind and body. By doing this, I will gain a new perspective that will give me more time to spend taking care of myself. I am the most valuable asset I have.*

### Focus and Be Resourceful

Because you are focusing on you and what you can do on your own, you will become more independent and resourceful. Why? When you're alone, especially if you're engaged in some project or adventure, you will learn independence and resourcefulness—because you have no choice. This will give you a new perspective on things. When you step back from the flow of events and social connections, you see things from a different vantage point and you just might come up with some fresh ideas you wouldn't have thought of otherwise.

Some people require more alone time than others. Many recent studies of introverts tell us that introverts process information and social interactions differently than extroverts. They even think differently! In order for introverts to use their many gifts effectively, they require more alone time.

What do you need to gain a new perspective on? How can you step back? Try at least one way to gain a new perspective today.

> *My time is limited and I will not waste it. I will allow my voice to be heard, and I will not listen to the voices of those who may doubt it. Today I will spend my time on me.*

## *It's Okay to Be Alone Sometimes*

Again, we sometimes don't realize how much energy our constant connection with other people requires and how this kind of multitasking causes stress and reduces our ability to concentrate. Removing the stimuli from connection to others improves concentration not just while you're alone but for some time afterward. Being alone can also help you to find your own voice

When you're dealing with others' interpretations of the world and with others' expectations and perceptions, it's hard to recognize your own! Time alone allows you to reduce the noise and "hear yourself think." What is your voice trying to tell you today? Is there a small whisper that you've been ignoring? What can you do right now to listen to that voice?

## DAY 7

> *My future is what matters. I will not focus on anything leading up to this point. Instead, I will only look toward the path that is leading me to my goals.*

## *The Power of Perspective*

When you put yourself in a space to get a different perspective, this bigger picture or more complete picture gives you more information for making decisions. What seemed enormous becomes less important. What you overlooked, including your own voice, becomes more important and clearer.

Wise managers and business owners understand alone time boosts creativity and productivity. Make certain both the physical structure and the workday schedule allow opportunities for the alone moments everyone in the organization needs, including you! You will be more effective and productive as will your employees.

# Procrastination Problems

This week's focus is on how to change your habits and become more productive.

Most entrepreneurs love making a to-do list. Whether it's neatly written on a notepad or typed into your mobile device, it makes you feel organized to write it down. Then you feel awful watching item after item go untouched as you slowly procrastinate throughout your day.

It's time to change and get to work on being more productive. Each day this week provides pointers on how to motivate yourself and stay on top of your tasks.

## DAY 1

> *Happiness is found in a positive attitude. I will not procrastinate in order to avoid confrontation. Instead I will find clarity in confrontation and remain happy.*

### Be Positive

It's easy to start happy, but you need a way to stay happy. Procrastination is most likely to happen if you feel sluggish, unwell, disappointed, or frustrated. Start by being healthy. The proper amount of sleep and the right foods will give you the physical and mental awareness to tackle the day.

Once you've got your body in check, work on boosting your emotional strength. Begin each day on a relaxed and happy note. Whether that means cutting out social media or resisting your e-mail for a couple of hours in the morning, take some time to focus on you and feel ready to conquer the coming day.

Now write down what you plan on cutting out of your life and for how long. Refer to that journal entry for the next seven days to remind yourself and be accountable to this promise.

## DAY 2

> *The world will be at a loss if I do not share my gifts with those I meet. In order to reach my full potential, I must share who I am with the world!*

### Let Others In

If you need a friend, or even a whole company to reach your goals, let someone else in on the game. Make the goals a priority and post them where everyone can see them. If your goals are primarily focused around yourself, use peer pressure to keep you motivated. Eric Barker at *Time* magazine suggests, "Give your friend $100. If you get a task done by 5 p.m., you get your $100 back. If you don't complete it, you lose the $100." Things will most certainly get done.*

Today should be the first day of your detox. Remember what you wrote down yesterday? How did your first day without that thing go? How do you feel when you are fasting? Write it down!

## DAY 3

> *It is my job today to light the world with my good thoughts. I refuse to let one negative thought enter my mind today!*

* http://time.com/2933971/how-to-motivate-yourself-3-steps-backed-by-science/

## Find Your Mantra and Make a Plan

"Just do it!" Nike's slogan is a great one. Create or copy a phrase to fit your goals. Post it on your computer, your bathroom mirror, your favorite book, or your forehead, if you must. Just see it, and see it often. When you find yourself in those moments when focus and attention are draining from you, repeat it to yourself and commit!

Now let's make a game plan. This is more than a checklist since your game plan can create a sense of accomplishment and direction. Half the battle is just getting started. List your short-term and long-term goals and the steps for each.

You'll most likely feel the most motivated in the morning; so tackle your hardest task for the day first and use that momentum to take on the rest of the day's tasks.

## DAY 4

> *I will not be jealous of the power that others may have. Instead, I will embrace that power and share mine with them so that we can become a force that will work together for good.*

## Embrace the Power of People

Surround yourself with people with similar interests and goals. You are bound to eat healthier if you spend time with healthy eaters; the same goes for exercise. If you familiarize yourself with successful, motivated people, then you are more likely to pick up their traits than they are yours. It's even as simple as communicating via LinkedIn or Facebook groups. Use these people to bolster your spirits when you are feeling down or to give you advice when you are stuck in the mud. You will be forever grateful to have a support system you can count on.

You are four days in! Have you stayed committed to your time away from that special thing? Write down why you've been successful or have failed thus far.

## DAY 5

> *When I feel defeated, I will rise up. When I*
> *feel that my problems are overwhelming, I will*
> *rise up. I will find happiness in how I rise.*

### Learn from Your Mistakes

Don't let mistakes or a bad day send you spiraling back to the couch of idleness. Take that opportunity to analyze what went wrong; it may be time to change your approach entirely. Step back, breathe, and remember—no one is perfect, but you sure can try.

Write down a story about a bad day and how you handled it. Then write down how you should have handled it. Then the next time you have a bad day, handle it the right way.

## DAY 6

> *Although I am good at finding patience with others, far*
> *too often I do not offer myself that same respect. Today*
> *I will be patient with myself and invest in who I am.*

### Treat Yourself

Just like any other training situation (yes, dogs included), if you don't reward yourself for your successes, you'll likely become burned out for lack of recognition. Start simple with, "If I complete tasks a, b, and c before noon, then I get ice cream for lunch." Build up to, "If we make x amount of money this month, I'm taking a vacation." Connect your goals to whatever things you like to do; let them support and sustain each other. You deserve a treat, but you also deserve to achieve success.

Write down what your treat will be. Make a promise to yourself to accept that treat if you complete your goals.

## DAY 7

> *My imagination is as great as my goals and I will never alter my dreams. I will use my imagination to grow big ideas, create magnificent dreams, and reach for the stars that I once thought were impossible to touch. I am capable of anything that I set my mind to.*

### Remember Your Successes

Once you've become more focused, treasure your accomplishments. Remind yourself of your successes—the small and the big. Write them down and keep them handy for those moments when you feel like you aren't going anywhere. Even remind yourself of where you've been for lack of trying and where you are today.

You can easily become your own biggest obstacle. But once you find and sustain the strength to be motivated, you can accomplish amazing things. Refer to your list on how to stay motivated when you find yourself wandering off the path to greatness. Take it from a master procrastinator: Start today, not tomorrow.

What is the number one thing that causes you to procrastinate? Make a note about it and also try to make a mental note that reminds you to slowly stop procrastinating.

# Boosting Your Bliss

It's never too late to choose a different path and a new life. Do you feel cornered by the decisions you've made in your life?

Most people at one point in their lives feel this way because they have low consciousness levels. From a very young age we are told what to do and what path to follow: Go to college, get a "useful" degree, find a high-paying job, buy a house and a car, get married, climb the ladder, and then retire. The problem with this is that it doesn't necessarily bring fulfillment and meaning into our lives.

## DAY 1

> *I will live every moment to its fullest and*
> *find happiness around every corner.*

### Show Gratitude

The good news is that it's never too late to take a step back and choose a new path and a new life. If you need to make a change in your life in order to be happy, you can use each of these tips to get you through each day until you've reached a new goal.

No matter what happens, always be positive about the different experiences and people you come in contact with throughout life. Each one of them has very valuable lessons to teach you. It goes without saying that the nicer you are, the more willing others are going to be to help you.

Write down one way that you can show gratitude to someone that you haven't. Then write down one person that shows gratitude to you and try to pay it forward next time you see them.

## DAY 2

> *My positive thoughts will defeat my negative thoughts. I have the ability to remain positive through any situation.*

### Get Rid of the Negative

We all want to be successful at work. So why are some people high achievers in the office while others never seem to get anything done? You have two options in order to find success at work: Stumble upon an ancient lamp with a genie, or set some real boundaries to avoid having way too much on your to-do list. Let's leave the genie option to Walt Disney and give you some tools to help you be happier and more productive.

Make a list of people who are an emotional drag on you and cut them out of your day. Start looking for new relationships that can inspire you and add some positivity into your life. Surround yourself with people who want you to succeed.

## DAY 3

> *My mind is a gift and I will not allow the weight of the world to take that from me. I will keep my mind clear and open. Stress will not define my world!*

### Take Care of Your Mind

Stress will kill your dreams. It's that simple. You have to have a clear and open mind or you may as well shut this book right now. You must take care of what you think in order to succeed.

Set some time in the morning and again before going to bed; then use this time to meditate and think about how you want to grow and contribute to the world. Really think about what will make you happy. Ask people who have been through the same obstacles for advice.

Write down the specific things that you want to meditate on and use those tomorrow morning when you try a short five-minute meditation. It's only five minutes!

## DAY 4

> *Not only do I need to keep my mind healthy, but I also need to nourish my body in a way that will help my mind to grow. I will remember to take care of myself today.*

### Take Care of Your Body

How was your meditation? Did you feel like you were more relaxed? Now that you are implementing some new strategies, I have another one for you. Set boundaries. You will begin to see they are the key to freedom and success. Undisciplined people look for a magical solution (like that genie in a bottle) to find work-life balance, but without boundaries, you will always be a slave to other people's agendas and unspoken expectations.

If your body can't support your mind, then you are never going to be successful. You are trying to be blissful here, and you can't do that if you are unhealthy. Try to implement at least 10 minutes of exercise into your regimen. Whether it's taking the stairs or walking instead of riding the shuttle, you can do this! Get your heart pumping and move forward. Write down what you plan on doing and stick to it!

## DAY 5

> *I am not content with mediocrity. I will strive to be the best, to win, and to refuse to accept defeat or allow others to succumb to the temptation of complacency.*

### Remember Their Crisis Is Not Your Emergency

Have you noticed how some people will do their best to suck you into their project dilemmas at work? When you make someone else's problem your problem, you are not helping them. You are enabling them.

Once your clients learn about your problem-solving skills, they will inundate your inbox and to-do list. You must be proactive and not divert these crisis creators in the heat of the moment. Clearly let people know in advance what you can and cannot take on, and leave their problems in their care.

Write down the things that you will no longer have to stress about if you start letting go of other people's problems. How much extra time will you have?

## DAY 6

> *Today I will please only those who respect me enough to maintain their boundaries with me. I cannot make everyone happy, and my happiness is stolen every day that I try.*

### Name Your Deal Breakers

Some people may not be able to clearly define a boundary they need to set. Here is a tool that might help. First, think of the person who is constantly dragging you away from your work to waste time dealing with his or her issues.

Make a quick list of "deal breakers"—the activities you are no longer going to engage in unless they somehow overlap with your own goals. These are the things that create even a twinge of anxiety when you are asked to do them. If you cannot define your own boundaries, how can you expect anyone else to know what they are? This activity will help you be ready to turn down the requests of others.

Take this one step further: Prepare a quick and kind "no" to their requests. For instance, "Thanks for the opportunity to help with your project, but I am already committed to a couple of important priorities of my own. You'll need to come back when my project is finished."

If your client wants to drop a deal breaker in your inbox, you can say something like this: "I would be happy to take on that priority. Which one of my other projects would you like me to deprioritize?" You will earn the respect of your client when they see you offer a kind, but firm no. You will no longer be overcommitted to extra work items and will have the time to enjoy the other relationships in your life more fully. Write down what your no will be like.

## DAY 7

> *My idea of a finished product may be different from someone else's. I will openly define my standards so that anyone who is dealing with me can understand where I am coming from.*

### Make a Social Contract

The best boundaries are clearly defined and set in advance. Create an understanding with your clients on what you would like to achieve, or what a successful completion of a project looks like.

You have to do this in advance. Begin the conversation by saying, "Here are the things most important to me," and then lay them out on the table.

Ask your clients for the same information. Unspoken and unmet expectations usually lead to huge confrontations. In this scenario, you can commit to a healthy work-life balance up front by stating, "My time with my family and friends is very important to me, and I expect to meet the demands of this project and my demands at home." Of course, no one can plan for every obstacle, but all expectations are spoken right at the outset, and people are able to balance all of their priorities without any surprises.

Today's assignment is to write a rough draft of your social contract in your journal. Don't worry about sharing it quite yet . . . just get it down on paper.

# Discipline and Determination

Success won't be achieved until your priorities have assumed the proper place in your life.

When looking at all the hard things you need to do to be successful, you have to keep in mind that the word "hard" is ambiguous. Does *hard* mean "difficult to understand," or does it mean "difficult to sustain"?

## DAY 1

> *Do something. Anything. Today I will get up and do something. It doesn't need to be an astounding feat, just one thing that will make a difference somewhere within the world. Today I will make a difference.*

### Discipline Yourself

The secrets to success have been published and discussed by successful people over and over again, from Norman Vincent Peale to Napoleon Hill. These secrets can be summarized as gaining self-knowledge and concentrating on making that self-knowledge work for you. That is a relatively easy concept to understand, but it is the second part that makes success "hard."

Perhaps the core of the problem is discipline, and the concept of delayed gratification. In order to reap the benefits, you have to continue to grow. What can you do to gain more knowledge in different areas? Is there a class you can take or a book you can read?

Write down one way that you can expand your knowledge and start the process toward making it happen.

## DAY 2

> *I will not be defined by labels. I am conscious of who I am, and I will live in the moment.*

### Maintain Your Presence

Make sure that you are always coming up with new ways to be noticed as a company and as a leader. From the company aspect, be sure that you are integrating social media into your advertising program, benchmarking other companies, and upholding a future plan. As a leader, stay innovative within all of your programs. Don't let your employees or teams get bored with the nine to five.

Write down one way that you have not been maintaining your presence as a company and one way that you have not been maintaining your presence as a leader. Now write the solution to each of those issues and implement both solutions.

## DAY 3

> *When I am in the right place at the right time, I will not be complacent. I will do something about it!*

### Know Your Requirements

If researching the implications of a product modification involves a massive Internet search, contacting business associates, and initiating training, then that is work that must be done. It isn't necessarily difficult to revise procedures regarding your own product line, but it might be tedious, especially if you would really rather be drinking a beer with your next-door neighbor and discussing the upcoming college football season.

Nevertheless, those who look to you for leadership need you to follow through and get them the proper information.

Success requires a sublimation of self to the requirements of others and your goals. It requires a passion for understanding your emotions, your pride, and your priorities so that you can schedule your time to spend it on what is necessary, not on what is necessarily pleasurable.

What are your priorities as an entrepreneur? Is it your current project or is there something long term that you are more passionate about? Is this a stepping-stone? Write down the answers to these questions and think about your priorities while you meditate for five minutes just as you learned last week. You are quickly implementing the things that you have learned into your daily routine.

## DAY 4

> *I can do anything, but I must take it one step at a time. Each day offers a new opportunity to manage one priority, one day at a time.*

### Assume Your Priorities

Success isn't achieved until your priorities have assumed the proper place in your life, and that means excluding those aspects of your life that involve achieving fleeting comforts. It means cultivating a higher level of growth in your mind and your aspirations.

When the quality of your commitment involves a dedication to respecting the contribution of those whom you rely on, then it becomes less an act of duty, and more a labor of love, to attend to the little things in your business that make it possible for your systems to function. The development of your own character involves participation.

What aspect of your life achieves fleeting comforts? What situation do you always fall back on? Can you remove that situation from your life so that you can focus on your priorities?

Write it down, but get serious here and stop falling back on that comfort. Replace it with a new habit.

## DAY 5

> *There is always an opportunity to dream higher and to think bigger. I am competing against myself and I want to win.*

### Recognize Your Dreams as the Revelations of Your Potential That They Are

Ask any child what he or she wants to be when they grow up, and you're liable to get some pretty wild answers—at least to the average adult, they'd seem wild. Think about it. What if an eight-year-old Sam Walton had told his father he wanted to be the world's largest retailer? What if a seven-year-old Yuri Gagarin had told his mother he wanted to be the first human in space? What if a five-year-old Barack Obama had told his kindergarten teacher he wanted to be president of the United States?

I don't know if a version of any of those conversations ever actually happened. But if they had, I suspect that in each case the listener would have responded in a kind, even encouraging manner. But I doubt they would have taken the possibility of the child actually realizing that dream very seriously. The reason for this is people's ability to dream big often diminishes as we grow older. If we can't dream big ourselves, it's hard for us to visualize the dreams of others.

What big dream have you pushed aside? Why? Did you give up or forget about it? Write a full-page testimony with artistic notes that states what that dream is. Dwell on it. Remember how it feels to dream. Remember that the next time you notice someone else dreaming.

# DAY 6

> *In order to reach my goal, I must visualize it, prepare for it, and be ready when the time arrives. Let the training begin!*

## Condition Yourself

Why do you suppose it is so hard for us to visualize our own dreams and the dreams of others? What is it that causes people to lose their ability to dream big and believe in those dreams as possibilities? The answer is our conditioning.

Most adults have been conditioned by a very powerful array of barriers. Throughout childhood we had parents, teachers, and other authority figures who repeatedly, albeit unintentionally, erected barriers in the paths of our dreams. They told us, "Don't do this," "Don't do that," "You can't do this," "You can't do that"—exerting an incredible amount of negative influence.

It's akin to what trainers do with circus elephants.

When they're very young, circus elephants are chained to a stake that's anchored very deep in the ground, thus preventing them from moving around at will. As strong as baby elephants are, they're unable to pull hard enough to pull the stake out of the ground. As the elephant grows up, he becomes accustomed to the idea that he can't pull free, even though the stake is now only driven a few feet into the ground. The animal has been conditioned, and this conditioning is much more powerful than the physical reality.

As you think about ways that you might be able to save someone with an elephant-like problem, write down the name of one person that you know of with a dream. It can be an employee, a family member, or a friend. Now write down what you can do to help that person visualize that dream. How can you make that dream a genuine possibility?

## DAY 7

> *Because I believe in what I am doing, I will not*
> *let anything stop me. Anything is possible.*

### You Can Pull This Off!

Remember that conditioned elephant we talked about yesterday? Here's a liberating fact: If a fully grown elephant would only try, he could easily pull that stake out of the ground with a tiny fraction of his adult strength!

And so can you.

As a child you may not have been able to overcome the negative influences you were subjected to. But as an adult, you have the power of autonomous choice. You have the power to rekindle those big childhood dreams, and to create new ones. So go ahead. Recognize your dreams as the revelations of your potential that they are. Refuse to allow any artificial barriers to deter you from rising to your full potential.

Make the commitment now to do whatever it takes to make those dreams happen. Write that commitment down. What is it that you have to commit to in order to get closer to that dream of yours? Is there a commitment that you can make to help that person we talked about yesterday too? I'll tell you, helping a person fulfill his or her dream is almost as inspiring as fulfilling your own!

# Summoning a Stronger Self

You don't have to ditch your principles to market yourself.

Some entrepreneurs, including some of the most determined and successful, are under the impression that they either don't have to bother with selling themselves, or that selling themselves is wrong.

## DAY 1

> *I am my first customer. If I'm not sold on my product or idea, how will I convince anyone else? I will focus on portraying the fact that I believe in myself!*

### Sell You, Not Out

There is a huge difference between "selling yourself" and "selling out." Selling yourself is simply marketing your skills and who you are, to both your clients and your organization. Selling out is trading in what makes you unique, like your standards or mission statement, for an immediate dollar or an advantage. See the difference?

Sometimes entrepreneurs think, "I don't have to be bothered with selling myself; I'll let my record do that." The problem is that only people familiar with your story know about your incredible skill set. For the rest of the world, you'll have to do some "on purpose" marketing. It's just a fact that in the business world today, marketing is required. You wouldn't design, patent, and create an awesome product and never advertise it.

Write down five ways that you can sell you. What makes you or your company and ideas special? Why are you unique?

## DAY 2

> *There is no time to fear failure. I will abandon any thoughts of failure and I will find success without a doubt!*

### Begin Keeping a Weekly Report of What You Do

As long as you never abandon what matters to you, you won't sell out. Begin by studying your personal mission statement. If you work for an organization, study its mission statement too. In some cases, you may have to juggle the two a bit to get a clear picture of who you are.

Start tracking your day-to-day activities on a weekly basis. Besides any duties required by your company, good things to include are times you spent mentoring or doing social work or whatever makes you unique. Put these reports in an e-mail or a simple newsletter format. Let the world know what you are doing. Send the people you want to impress a weekly report of what you are doing.

Start out by designing your weekly report tonight and make a list of the people you are going to share it with.

Use a blog or a platform like LinkedIn to blog about your industry or profession. Become a thought leader. Decide on one platform where you want to publish and create an account today. Write down your username and password in your journal so you don't forget them.

## DAY 3

> *My image is important to me and I want people to remember who I am. I will craft my image daily and be sure to set a steadfast example for those I lead.*

*Work on Ways to Sell Yourself*
- **Update your public profile.** Change your profile picture and update your work status on all social media. Sell yourself by being current and providing the world with up-to-date information. When possible, find a way to display your personal creed. Write down your personal creed in your journal and talk to someone about creating a unique typography or graphic design for it.
- **Frame your degrees and certifications.** What better way to "sell yourself" than to display what you have already achieved? What achievements do you want to include? Write down which specific ones that you want to display and start the process of getting them ready to display.

## DAY 4

> *There is a peace that is found in volunteering.*
> *Today I will dedicate some of my time to finding*
> *opportunities where I can selflessly help others.*

*Become Active in the Community and Take Some Risks*
Look for opportunities to join local nonprofit boards and local chamber of commerce committees; find opportunities to speak at local civic clubs. Write down one nonprofit that you are interested in and look it up online. Make sure you check out the different ways that you can volunteer.

It's not always easy to spend your time volunteering and sometimes it can be a gamble, but if you want to win big, you'll have to risk big. In addition to volunteering in order to sell yourself, you have to make sure that you don't forget who you are along the way. People who achieve brilliant things outside of the office get praised. You'll have to play the balancing game if you choose this method to sell yourself.

Remember that you don't have to negotiate with your principles to stand out in the crowd. Volunteer in an area that you are actually passionate about. With some skill, you can sell your dream, your product, and even yourself while helping others at the same time. Where might you be able to volunteer? How will that help you when it comes to your actual job? Make some notes in your journal and visualize what is going to work best for you.

## DAY 5

> *Competition is fierce. I will be resilient when it comes to staying one step ahead of the competition. It is my job to continue to keep my company on top.*

### Use Social Media to Level the Playing Field

As a business owner, you have to find ways to compete even with the big guys. Size matters, right? Bigger is always better (just ask Texas), and small means weak. (Don't tell David or Goliath!) We all know that size can matter the other way, too, and there are several techniques that will help a small business compete with big businesses.

Social media can level the playing field. No matter how much money is in your marketing budget, you still only have one corporate Twitter account. Sure, you could be like Cisco whose social media page shows no fewer than 15 Twitter accounts, but your message and meaning will likely be fractured. Set up camp in a few key areas and then shine. Where do you think that you can make your business shine the most? Write it down and explore it online today!

## DAY 6

> *Learning to adapt is something that I must perfect. I can adapt and I will. Whatever the job is, I can do it.*

### Adaptability Is Your Advantage

Small companies are also able to pivot in the marketplace than a large company can. Witness the fortunes of mighty Blockbuster Video when a startup company began "renting" unlimited movies through the mail with a small monthly fee. Soon after, Netflix began streaming movies over the Internet, an extremely quick pivot into a burgeoning marketplace, and where is Blockbuster nowadays? It tried to keep up but was slow to turn the ship. Its sheer size prevented it from making a full tack, resulting in bankruptcy. Small is light and quick.

How can you take advantage of a current event to pivot your company or product? Where can you make sure that you get noticed? Read some current event business stories online and write down the ones that are relevant to your business.

## DAY 7

> *The success of my company depends on the happiness and loyalty of my customers. I will take time to understand my customer in depth today and in a way that will connect us through more than just a product or service.*

### Customer Service Is Your Edge

Finally, most large companies cannot compete with small businesses when it comes to customer service. There are exceptions to this rule (Zappos jumps to mind), but the company has a playbook that is wide open for all to see and copy. And really, we all win when customer service and support are exceptional. Give your customers something to rave about when they contact your company and they will gladly spread the word. When you're a small company, you can get to know your customers on an individual basis. Take that, Goliath!

How does your small company do it better than the big guys? Write down five ways that you outshine the giants within your industry. Be confident.

# Managing Management

If you can't manage your own life, how can you expect to manage other people? Think about it for a second. Don't all the business management tips you have come across so far pretty much come down to answering that question in one way or another?

As business owners and entrepreneurs, one of our most important desires is creating a place where people enjoy coming to work. Take it from me, when you are looking at how to build a great workplace, it can be hard to know where to begin. Don't get overwhelmed.

## DAY 1

> *Efficiency is more important than activity when it comes to my business as a whole. Sometimes, things have to be done slowly in order to be done properly. Today, I will find patience in efficiency.*

### Quirky Business Management

How do you go about managing a business project that requires managing the personalities, quirks, character issues, and emotional pendulums of others?

Business management is about more than just telling underlings what to do and when to do it. It is about more than asking coworkers to politely get back in the game instead of furtively tweeting away about whatever life event took place the night before. Now that you know what your goals are and understand the importance of teamwork and motivation, it's time to work on the specifics of your management skills. These business management tips essentially boil down to getting you to look at how you manage yourself as a means of learning to manage others.

Think about what managing others means to you. What do you think are the key attributes that make a successful manager? Write down some of those qualities.

## DAY 2

> *It is time for me to learn that how I use my time will dictate my success. Managing my time is something that I will do better today.*

### Exploit Time

Are you a morning person or night owl? Managing life at 10:30 a.m. may be a breeze for you, but you have trouble remembering if you kissed the kid goodnight or not by 10:30 p.m. at night. Take a serious look at how well you manage your life through different periods of the day to get a better understanding of the reality that everybody's internal clock is set to a different time zone. Managing others will become easier and more effective if you make the effort to find out when the people you are counting on do their best work.

For instance, if you've got two people who do their best work early in the day and two people who do their best work in the afternoon, project management begins by assigning the introductory elements to the morning people and the secondary elements to those who are just coming into their own after lunch.

Write down the differences between some of your employees and where you think they are best utilized. Do you need to change your approach?

## DAY 3

> *My goals have deadlines and I must adhere to them!*
> *While some goals may seem decades away, I will still strive*
> *to complete them in a timely and efficient manner.*

### Set Goals

Yep, more goal-setting. The value of setting goals that are strictly defined cannot be overestimated when it comes to managing a team. Do you set goals for yourself? You're running a business, right? So, yes, of course you do.

If you manage goals for yourself effectively, then you intuitively know that effective management of others is based on ensuring that everybody is aware of the strictly defined overall goal as well as the strictly defined goal for their individual part in the process. If people know the goal and the mission, and are given the tools to succeed, your success will skyrocket. The key is setting goals for everyone in your organization that are tough but achievable.

Remember some of those goals that you set last month? How are they looking? Do you need to modify them now that you are learning more about your team? Revisit those goals and make a list of any that might need to be changed or adapted.

## DAY 4

> *I will emphasize the positive every single day.*
> *Whether I am miserable or strong is up to me and*
> *what I decide to put emphasis on. When I emphasize*
> *the positive consistently, I will reward myself!*

### Set Rewards

Think about the way you manage your personal life. You clearly set goals for yourself, right? When you achieve those goals, you make a point of not rewarding yourself, right? Of course not! Who does that?

What you probably don't do is reward yourself monetarily every time you achieve a goal. Setting rewards for accomplishing strictly defined goals doesn't have to mean an actual cash payment.

Rewards can range from a new desk chair (with four working wheels!), to a day off from work, to tickets for a ballgame. Be creative in organizing your reward system and you will find that managing other people becomes much easier. There is more to life than money. More business owners need to understand this.

Make a list of some rewards that you might be able to offer your team.

## DAY 5

> *There is a way to make a meeting successful. Today I will find a way to do just that! I will manage my meetings in a way that benefit my company, not my ego.*

### Manage Your Meetings

You know what? You hate meetings. The people you manage hate meetings. Everybody hates meetings.

Unfortunately, you can't manage a business of more than one person without holding meetings. What you can do is take a tip from the way you manage your life away from the office. Do you hold a meeting to discuss who will take out the garbage? Do you hold a meeting to discuss what to have for dinner? Maybe, but probably not.

The point is you don't need to call an official meeting when you can easily provide all the particular information in the form of a report or e-mail or conference call or just, you know, dropping in on people and talking. People pay more attention to their e-mails than they do to meetings. How can you minimize time spent in meetings? Write down some of your ideas and implement them into your schedule. Then, after a week or two, come back and make a note of whether or not those ideas worked for you.

## DAY 6

> *My company will be aligned with my purpose.*
> *By doing this, my employees become passionate*
> *about our purpose and will help us to grow.*

### Understand Your Purpose

Knowing your purpose is fundamental to building a great place to work. When a company has a firm grasp on the reason they are in business, it provides individual employees with a sense of belonging to something bigger than themselves. Yes, your employees want to earn a fair wage, but most people do not get out of bed to simply collect a check. In order to create excitement and deep satisfaction, people want to know their work truly matters and makes a difference. Your company will be able to find employees who resonate with your purpose.

Start with *why* and then move outward from there.

## DAY 7

> *I will define my company culture. When there*
> *are days that feel overwhelming, I will not let*
> *stress change who I am. I will uphold a culture of*
> *positivity and strength, even on bad days.*

### Hire for Culture

A famous quote attributed to legendary management guru Peter Drucker said that culture eats strategy for breakfast. It's true. You can create the most ingenious strategy and have a group of people with incredible skill sets, but it won't matter unless they fit your culture.

Most people really want to work hard and do their best (of course, there are exceptions to this rule). They want to show up and complete the work set in front of them. However, if they do not have the same work ethic, values, and beliefs about business as you—they will not succeed.

It may be time to evaluate the cultural fit of your employees. How? Communicate your values clearly . . . and often. It may dawn on you, and your employees at that point, why you (and they) are so frustrated.

Write down how you can communicate better. Do you recognize anyone that is not going to join the culture at your company? Write the name down. Be honest. Find a graceful way to sever ties if that employee has no intention of joining the culture of your workplace. More important—hold tightly to those who do want to join you; they will pay off in spades.

# *Personality Profiles*

How do you manage different personality types to accomplish the mission?

The workplace is a melting pot of personalities—no surprise there! All types of employees must work together and are expected to overcome personal differences to reach a common goal. But ethics, cultural norms, and temperament can sometimes cause friction.

## DAY 1

> *My personality will define me. Whether I am shy, outgoing, or funny, I will find a way to use my personality as an asset. Who I am is defining who I will be. It's up to me to embrace it!*

### The Personality Problem

Let's discuss temperament. All employee groups will exhibit two main types: introverts and extroverts. Each type can interact very differently in the workplace. One may be better suited for leadership than the other.

But can you always tell which is which? All employees deserve and appreciate respect for who they are. Acknowledge the introverted or extroverted traits that you think you've observed. You may later find you have defined the person in error. Many true introverts have learned to act like extroverts in certain situations and vice versa.

Make a list of some of the introverts and extroverts on your team. We'll check later and see if you were right or wrong.

## DAY 2

> *I will learn to be outgoing in situations where that trait is a necessity. I may not always feel comfortable, but I understand I must adapt to each situation. I can do this!*

### Extroverts

People who are naturally outgoing never seem to meet a stranger. Everyone is a potential client, or better yet, a potential friend. An extrovert will seem to volunteer for everything that comes along. These are the employees who will work on several committees at a time, even if the committees have little in common.

They involve themselves socially with everyone who will have them. They instigate personal discussions and often become the social directors for the department. Extroverts sound like wonderfully interactive people, don't they? They can be—but a dark side may also emerge.

Think about yourself. Are you an extrovert? Why or why not? Write down your reasons.

## DAY 3

> *When it is time to sit back and be quiet, I will learn to do so. I can control my emotions and remain calm in any situation.*

### The Dark Side of Extroverts

So, welcome to the dark side. Extroverts can emotionally overpower a client who prefers to remain "strictly business," causing mistrust. If this is you or one of your employees, you must learn to moderate this tendency according to the client's needs. In addition, extroverts can burn out quickly when trying to impress others or earn respect through overcommitment. This manager must learn balance and when to say no.

Proper boundaries are a must if this individual is to maintain the respect of others. Sometimes an extrovert is not always taken seriously. Is there an extrovert on your team that might not be taken seriously because of his or her personality? Do you need to take a closer look? Think about it and write down how you feel.

## DAY 4

> *I will learn to acknowledge those around me even when I am busy or frustrated. By allowing others to see that I am listening to them even in times of trouble, I will further gain their trust and respect.*

### Introverts

This personality type often prefers to work in solitude. They may even get angry if interrupted. They acknowledge the lives of others but don't enter social discussions. You may think that they don't like their co-workers because they rarely show up at gatherings that are not business related. These employees tend to wait until an assignment is refused by others before stepping up. A coworker might feel as if the introvert resents taking on the burden.

It sounds as if introverts would make poor leaders, doesn't it? They can be, but you might look at it another way. There just might be a bright side to this personality type.

Do you have an introverted personality? Have you figured out exactly where you stand yet? What can you do to take advantage of your personality type?

**DAY 5**

> *When I am given a task, I will focus on it*
> *until I have successfully completed it. In any*
> *situation, I can concentrate on my goals.*

### The Bright Side of Introverts

The bright side is that introverts can have impressive powers of concentration and problem-solving. When this manager presents his or her plan, it will usually be detailed and well thought-out. Introverts can act as a buffer or diplomat, given that they tend to observe behavior from a distance. This manager can often explain differing points of view without becoming emotionally involved. Introverts often become effective leaders, not in spite of but because of the fact that they don't push themselves forward. They tend to have a realistic view of their abilities and the patience to figure out the job as it progresses.

But what actually constitutes an extrovert or introvert? It's quite simple. An extrovert recharges by being with people, while an introvert recharges by being alone.

Have you figured out how to be in control of your personality? Are you noticing any differences or that you are treated a certain way because of your personality type? Write down how you feel about it.

**DAY 6**

> *If I meet a client, employee, coworker, or customer*
> *who is loud and obnoxious, I will treat that person*
> *with the same respect that I would like. I will find*
> *a way to communicate in any situation.*

### Approaching the Extrovert

An extrovert would often rather meet with people and start the day off running. He or she will tend to be more productive when allowed to bounce ideas off others during the workday. Schedule regular brainstorming sessions or encourage an extrovert to engage with other people as needed. An extrovert may want to explain every detail of his or her plan immediately. Acknowledge an extrovert's good ideas in front of peers without allowing his or her enthusiasm to hijack the meeting.

Think about ways that you can learn to utilize the extroverts on your team. Does this change any of the original goals that you set for your team? Write down the answer.

## DAY 7

> *If I am having trouble getting the right information from someone, I will try to approach the situation differently. I will speak in a way that makes the person feel comfortable and able to share his or her thoughts.*

### Approaching the Introvert

An introvert generally prefers to ease into the workday by sorting and planning alone for the first half hour. That person may want to retreat strategically during the day. Allow the introvert to schedule "alone time," or encourage the person to use a "do not disturb" signal when necessary. An introvert may not be comfortable speaking up when a general call for ideas is given. Ask him or her directly (possibly before the meeting) to share any suggestions.

Finally, encourage extroverts and introverts to work together. It's sometimes a bit uncomfortable, but each has strengths that will improve the professional development of the other as well as contribute value to the project.

Do you have unique ways to manage the personalities in your office? Write them down and share them with others!

# Evolution Essentials

Now that you are learning how to effectively manage and cultivate your team, let's talk about adding to it. Every small business has to evolve and grow, and usually that means bringing in some qualified help. After many hiring disasters, my partner and I learned to hire better.

This week reveals important strategies that will help you find the perfect person to fill the job while your company finds growth, and it will increase your ability to be an effective interviewer.

## DAY 1

> *It's my job to be careful how I present myself. I will be aware of the attitude that I am projecting and be sure that I am working with people who have needs that I can meet and vice versa.*

### Blind Ambition

When we first started our company, we had no idea what we were doing in terms of hiring and it showed when we started growing at a crazy pace. After many hiring disasters—including an incident with the police and several poor choices that could have cost us everything—we learned to hire better and take our time.

Make sure the job description is clear to the applicant with enough information about the job. Include necessary skills, duties, type of business, location, benefits, and opportunity for advancement. Be as clear as you possibly can to try and weed out a few unqualified applicants.

Make sure you remember to prescreen each applicant to eliminate unsuitable or overqualified applicants early. You don't want to waste your time interviewing that "really nice guy" who wants to be paid way more than you can afford. Do your homework before you interview.

Start planning your job description today. Make a list of what you are looking for.

## DAY 2

> *Some questions need not be complicated. My task today is to focus on the little things. The simple questions may result with the most confounding answers.*

### Interviewing Essentials

The key to interviewing prospective employees is gaining enough knowledge about the applicant so that you can award the position to the most qualified candidate.

Make sure you explain your purpose as the interviewer and go over company policies. Encourage the applicant to ask questions and answer them with more questions. The more you know, the better—even if it seems redundant.

Don't hire friends or relatives who aren't qualified. This is where your integrity will come into play. You must treat everyone the same, giving equal opportunity to all who apply. You must find the best employee for the position and any emotional connections will hinder your ability to see each perspective employee equally.

What types of questions are you planning to ask? Start narrowing them down today.

## DAY 3

> *Even when I feel the need to ask a question that is outside of my plan, I will refrain and stick to my own personal guidelines. I must stay on track during my conversations with potential employees in order to be objective.*

### The Gritty Guidelines

Finding the right employee involves much more than asking a few questions. You need to follow certain guidelines to get the information you need to make the best choice. Be aware and try to avoid monotony.

Allow the applicant to do most of the talking, and the interview should take 60 to 90 minutes to complete. Don't fall into the trap of doing all of the talking because of nervousness or tension. You need to get the facts on this prospective employee as well as insight into his or her personality.

Focus on asking the applicant what he or she would like to improve on. Most prospective employees find it much easier to discuss improving themselves than admitting they lack essential qualities or skills. Decide whether or not those skills are ones that you can wait for improvement on. If you can't wait, then you know this person may not be a good fit for your company.

Make a list of the qualities that you are looking for in your new employee. This is for your own personal use, so be specific.

## DAY 4

> *I'm going to remember to be real today.*
> *I will avoid being false at all costs.*

### Help Me, Help You

Speak softly. This encourages applicants to take center stage. Give them the opportunity to speak as much as they need to. This may be especially difficult for you if you have that extroverted personality that we talked about last week.

Use ideas from the resume or application to form an outline for your questions. Read your applicant's resume *before* the interview. Just because you've already got the job doesn't mean that you are allowed to forgo your homework. Finding good employees is hard, but if you want to find the good ones, you have to put in the work too.

Once you've done your research, come up with a few specific questions for each applicant.

## DAY 5

> In all seriousness, stopping the seriousness
> for a minute is okay. Today I will take time
> to talk about the simple things in life.

### The Power of Small Talk

Spend a few minutes in small talk. Depending on your personality type, this may be difficult for you or very easy, but it's important. Does the applicant have a favorite sports team? What are his or her hobbies? Express a real interest in getting to know them so that they feel comfortable when you start asking the real questions.

Look responsive by raising one eyebrow, or smiling slightly. Nodding your head will invite the prospective employee to elaborate. Again, if you are introverted, this may really be tough for you. However, if you want to learn the most about your prospect, that person needs to feel comfortable.

Make a list of small talk questions that you might want to use with your applicants.

## DAY 6

> *I will focus on finding employees who are ready*
> *to maintain my company culture. It's up to me to*
> *find people who will work with my ideals.*

### Reference Rules

Check references by calling on the phone, and double-check the negative responses to make sure the reference just didn't like the applicant for personal reasons that had nothing to do with work. Once again, do your homework. This is just as important of a choice for you as it is for the applicant.

Ask questions like, "Tell me about yourself. Why are you here at this particular company? Tell me about your last job." Sincerely try to get inside the applicant's head. Understand where the person is coming from and why he or she wants to work for you.

Spend time reviewing the work history of your applicants and make sure that each one is still a good fit for you now that you've come up with some questions. Maybe a few of them have already been answered in the cover letters or on the applicants' resumes.

## DAY 7

> *In order to find people who will fit my company*
> *culture, I will learn to be aware of their personality*
> *traits and judge them by more than a resume. I will*
> *take the time to get to know everyone I speak with.*

### Take Your Time

Look for these traits: flexibility, readiness, punctuality, high energy level, and a problem solver. These are traits of a leader.

Do not make your decision to hire the prospective employee "on the spot." Give yourself time to reach the right decision, and allow all of the candidates an equal shot. Go into each interview with an open mind and you will find the prospective employee that you are looking for. Write down one thing that you might be closed-minded about and be brutally honest. Now try and figure out how you can be more open-minded about the subject.

If you incorporate the strategies that you have learned this week into your hiring process, you will be successful in employing the right person for the job. You will have a win-win result for both you and your newest employee, and you will have gained some good, practical experience at being an effective and successful interviewer.

# *Creating Content Cubicles*

If we've talked about this once, we've talked about it a million times.—if you do not have happy employees, your business will absolutely not thrive. So, let's go back and see if you are keeping up with the cubicles that are filled with members of your team, and decide what other risk-free rewards and actions you can use in order to have a thriving office.

It's Management 101, but as entrepreneurs and managers we often forget to reward people for a job well done. Maybe you are just starting out or your business can't afford to give costly raises, bonuses, or extravagant gifts. Let's take a look at some ways you can show your employees that you care this week. Try to practice the example that is provided every day this week. Write down how your employees reacted and what their productivity levels were like.

## DAY 1

> *I will sincerely show gratitude to everyone that I speak with today. I am blessed beyond measure and I will make sure that others know that I appreciate them.*

### Show Appreciation
You can reward your employees by simply showing your appreciation for them and all they do.

1. **An exceptional reward:** Give your hardworking employee an unexpected paid day off work.
2. **That awesome parking space:** If you are able, allocate parking spots to those who deserve a reward.
3. **A personal note:** Leave a handwritten note on your employee's desk telling him or her what a good job they have been doing and how much you appreciate it.

Do each of these things today and write down how you felt about it. Record if you got any positive responses.

## DAY 2

> *Happy employees feel appreciated! Reward the efforts that other people put in to help you and your business. It's important to remember you didn't get here completely on your own.*

### Reward Everyone

Rewards for everyone in the office can include:

1. **Fun time and team-building:** Allot a few hours every month to having fun. Playing games can be a great stress reliever in addition to being a rewarding break.
2. **Food:** Bring donuts or a healthier alternative to the office, buy pizza for lunch, or maybe stock the kitchen once a week with snacks for everyone. Use office time whenever possible. Some employees don't want to use their time off to celebrate their business successes.

Choose one of these rewards and implement them today. How did it work? Were your employees grateful?

## DAY 3

> *When I praise my employees, they will want to be more productive. I will spend time today making sure that my employees and coworkers know that I am thankful for them.*

### Give Recognition

One way to reward your employees is by recognizing them. Some ways to do this are:

1. **The good write-up:** Acknowledge employees who have done exemplary work by including a small article about them in the company newsletter or blog or on social media.
2. **Employee of the month:** Put an Employee of the Month policy in place. You can reward someone once a month with a prime parking place or by putting the employee's picture on the wall.
3. **Simple gifts:** The key to rewarding someone with a gift is knowing the person well enough to present a gift that is meaningful. Giving a gift that shows you have paid attention to your employee is often more impressive than something that costs a lot of money.

Write down one employee that you feel deserves one of the three rewards above and make it happen. Write down why you chose that employee and what the reward was.

## DAY 4

> *My relationship with my customers is meaningful. In order to be successful, I have to be sure that my customer knows that I need and appreciate him or her. Today I will make sure my customer understands that.*

### Be Transparent

Don't be fooled by the phrasing—it sounds a lot easier than it actually is. As a manager, you have one job that supersedes all others and that is gaining the trust of your employees. It takes time, work, and dedication.

This is probably the best advice I can give you. Be transparent; be honest. As long as you're up front with your employees, there's nothing you can do to completely lose their trust. I don't mean being transparent on Mondays, by the way. It's an everyday commitment. The point is to get your employees to believe in you.

Come up with one brutally honest action that you can incorporate into your office and do it. Write it down and make sure that you stop sugarcoating and start seeing results.

## DAY 5

> I will not make promises that I cannot keep. If something is unattainable, I will not tell my employees or customers that it is. My integrity means more than empty promises.

### Deliver on Promises

If you ever promise anything to employees, make sure that you deliver. This can be something small, like promising a pizza party if you receive a certain amount of positive reviews on Yelp that month. It can also be a bit more serious, like promoting employees after promising an advancement opportunity.

It's not hard for employees to tell if you're looking out for their best interests. This includes everything from giving them the right training to sponsoring a good health insurance plan. If an employee is sick, then tell him or her to feel better and to take time off to recuperate.

Write down a best-interest plan to incorporate into your employee handbook. It doesn't have to be on a large scale, but simply having that little addendum will inspire your employees and reiterate the fact that you are looking out for them.

## DAY 6

> *There will be weeds in the bunch, but as long as I*
> *am a good manager and I appreciate my employees,*
> *they will be motivated to work for me efficiently.*

### Recognize Hard Work

At the end of the day, employees want to know that management notices their hard work. A simple "thank you" can go a long way as long as it's sincere and has good timing. Don't underestimate the motivation that comes from employee recognition.

Think about new and innovative ways, other than what we've already learned, to recognize your employees for all of their hard work.

Come up with three new ways that you've never heard of before and write them down.

## DAY 7

> *I want happy employees, not just productive*
> *employees. I'm willing to put just as much effort in*
> *to their happiness as I am their productivity.*

### Invest in Them

If you invest in your employees, it shows that you believe in them and want them to stay with the company. Investing in employee training shows that you don't just care about product—you also care about staff members' personal and professional development.

Do your employees trust you? Make a list of some things that you can do to gain their trust.

# Demolishing Drama

Office drama is just what the name implies: a drama. The workplace is the stage, and there are actors, a script, a plot, a supporting cast, and an audience. You may try to stay off the stage, but sometimes you get pulled in. Your time is consumed, you become less productive, and sometimes you can even face consequences because of your involvement. It's just not worth it! It's important to understand the difference between normal tensions among employees that are generated by demanding deadlines and workloads, and office drama that is self-created conflict, resulting in unnecessary workplace stress.

How do you stop the production?

## DAY 1

> No matter what happens when I am not around,
> the activity among my employees directly affects me
> and the morale of my company. I will be aware of
> the situations that happen within my workplace.

### No More Drama

Whether you're the boss, the manager, or an employee, we've all dealt with office drama. Office dramatics may range from mildly childish to the sort that threatens to sabotage careers. All office drama reduces productivity by diverting energy from projects and deadlines, and breeds resentment among all employees—even those who do not actively participate in it.

It's not easy to sit back and watch the drama unfold, knowing exactly what's about to happen. Maybe you think you can stop it if you get involved. Maybe you want to know the story and it's hard for you to stay out of it. Sometimes you might even feel left out if you don't take a part in the show. If you feel like you are punching into a movie set every morning instead of your place of business, the rest of this week provides tips on how to deal with the actors who stage it.

Write down the most dramatic event that you've had to deal with and how you handled it. What could you have done differently?

## DAY 2

> *There will be drama. Human beings are not perfect.*
> *However, when there is conflict within my company, I*
> *will not ignore it. I will deal with it and move on.*

### The Antagonist

Because this sort of self-created conflict doesn't originate in the workplace, it's less about work-related conflict, and usually more about preexisting, individual personality issues that are imported into the workplace. Employees can make a conscious decision to leave their personal problems at home, but it's not so easy to leave their personalities there.

Watch for the person I call "the Antagonist." This person engages in outright intimidation and verbal abuse. These actors are insecure in their workplace roles and mask their uncertainty by behaving in overly aggressive and controlling ways.

How to deal with the Antagonist: Give this person something to be certain about. Set an absolute zero policy against verbal and physical intimidation and then back it up. If the Antagonist still fails to respect boundaries, document his or her behaviors, and make sure there are consequences for his or her actions.

135

Can you think of an antagonist in your office? Write down what you can do to tame them and implement it!

## DAY 3

> *If I am the cause of the drama in my company, I will find a way to stop it. If the workload is too heavy or the demands too great, it's my job to figure out a way to lessen that load. My employees' happiness comes first.*

### The Victim

On the opposite end of the spectrum is the tragic martyr of the office. This person's script revolves around constant complaints and nothing is ever the Victim's responsibility. Typically, the Victim plays the supporting role to the Antagonist, who cannot act out his or her role without a Victim. Unfortunately, if there is no real Antagonist present, the Victim will create one.

How to deal with the Victim: Sincerely express your regret over the trials the Victim is enduring, and then firmly excuse yourself by stating you are busy with an important project. The Victim's mentality is fed by participation. Don't jump on stage with the person.

How'd it go with the Antagonist yesterday? Write down that person's reaction and whether it helped. Now make a note of what you can do to desensitize the Victim.

## DAY 4

> *I will not participate in any gossip nor will I tolerate those who do. Employee happiness is key, but blatant disregard and disrespect for my company or the employees within it is something that I'm not okay with.*

## The Subplotters

The next type is the Subplotter, who can be identified by his or her incessant gossip. This is not to be confused with idle water-cooler chat. The Subplotters are those constant town criers of the workplace who are actually covert Antagonists. Their scripts are slanderous, undermine others, and serve to give the Antagonist and the Victim their stage cues.

How to deal with the Subplotters: When the Subplotter attempts to reveal a juicy plot twist in the drama, calmly ask why the person is revealing the gossip to you. Reassuring the Subplotter that you intend to verify the story with the parties in question often thwarts the person.

How's the Victim doing? Did your idea work? Write down a specific question that you will ask a Subplotter should you come across one.

## DAY 5

> *While there may be backlash, I'll avoid getting*
> *sucked into any drama that does not involve me.*
> *Unless it's necessary for me to intervene, I will let*
> *my employees work things out on their own.*

## The Supporting Cast

Members of the Supporting Cast inadvertently feed office drama by becoming sympathetic to the stories of all the major players.

How to deal with the Supporting Cast: Gently remind yourself and others that you are in the office to focus on work-related tasks. While emotional sensitivity is required for daily work-related stresses, no one has to play the role of therapist to self-created office drama.

Do you have feeders in your workplace? What can you feed them with instead of drama? Write down three things.

## DAY 6

> *Sitting back and watching the drama unfold like a television show is almost as bad as participating in it. I will avoid all forms of participation in workplace drama that I cannot control.*

### The Audience

These are employees who have no active role on stage, yet who may hesitate to set boundaries with office drama-makers. The Audience may fear appearing uncooperative when they confuse office drama roles with being a team player.

How to deal with the Audience: Make it known to the Audience they need not give a standing ovation to those acting out their personal drama on the office stage. All drama-makers need an Audience. When the Audience isn't interested, the show closes.

How can you encourage the Audience to stop watching the show? Write down three ways.

## DAY 7

> *People are not always nice or cooperative when asked to modify their behaviors or habits. I will find a way to moderate drama that needs to be controlled without singling anyone out.*

### The Cool Head

The overarching primary tactic for dealing with office drama is to keep your cool. Drama, inside the office and out, requires emotional reaction to keep the plot moving forward. A little responsiveness goes a long way toward pulling the curtain down.

How do you deal with office drama? Has it affected your company and your ability to build a great team? Answer the first question and then think of new ways that you can avoid it and test them out today.

# Support, Shake, and Succeed

Frame your mission around how the business will serve others. A successful entrepreneur isn't concerned only with the bottom line. Profit is important, of course, as it drives how a business operates. However, to become a leader in your niche, you have to impact others, whether on the local or the global level. When you successfully frame your mission around how your business will serve others, you will have what it takes to impact people and communities, and probably a pretty successful business as well.

## DAY 1

> *I will think of how I can serve others today. While earning money is an important aspect of my company, serving my customer base is more important.*

### Serving Others

When you first dreamed up an idea for your business—whether you planned to sell a product or a service—what sparked that idea?

Chances are, you saw a problem that you could solve. Somewhere along the way, many entrepreneurs shift their focus to how their ideal customers can serve their business and end up spending their time chasing down those elusive "A+" clients.

However, if you keep your goals focused on serving others with your business, then the ideal clients will come to you. The real question is: How do you implement this practice of serving others?

## DAY 2

> *Visualizing my goals will help me progress toward them. In addition, I will set smaller goals to reach along the way and to keep me motivated. I will accomplish one small goal today!*

### Visualization

Meditation, daydreaming, visualizing, imagining—whatever you call it, spending 10 or 15 minutes each morning thinking about how your business can serve others will help you keep this perspective in mind. Try to imagine someone coming into your store or visiting your website. Create a narrative for him or her. Why did this potential customer come to you? What do you offer that no one else can? Visualize helping this potential customer, as though you had all the money in the world and making a sale was not important.

The days of becoming the type of salesperson who can "sell ice to an Inuit" are over. Successful businesses serve their clients, not the other way around. Keep this meditation in mind as you work throughout the day, and you will find ideal clients repeatedly drawn to your product or service.

## DAY 3

> *I need goals in my personal life as well as my professional life. They are meaningful and important to me. I am not guided by others and I, alone, am responsible for reaching those goals.*

## The Meaning of Success

What does success mean to you? If you wish to impact people, communities, and the world, then your definition of success should include how your business serves others—how it fulfills their needs.

After your morning meditation, write out your business goals for that day. How will your company serve others? Write down some realistic goals and outline action steps to achieve them. Then share them with your team so that they understand the goals and objectives.

## DAY 4

> *I will not be satisfied when I reach one goal or find one dream. Dreaming at all hours of the day is something that will fuel my motivation toward being successful.*

## Hit the Proverbial Open Road

I was in a hotel gym the other day riding a stationary bike to get a little exercise. I needed the workout after a long flight. But it made me think, what if I had to ride this bike every day? I would lose interest. I would probably stop exercising. This kind of experience takes all the joy out of a real ride into the countryside. Sure, it's comfortable to a degree, but you'll never experience the thrill of taking on those hills like the cycling "beast" you are and you won't feel the wind blowing through your hair on the downward glide.

The same is true in business. It's not the folks on the stationary bikes who get the big rewards. For real success in business, you'll have to hit the proverbial open road, take off the training wheels, and commit to reaching beyond your comfort zone.

What's the goal? PROGRESS. Comfort is the enemy—can you defeat it? Sure you can! Start by creating some excitement and momentum in your business. Write down your plan. Shed those comfortable meetings and the status quo operations. Shake things up and achieve real progress.

## DAY 5

> *There will be mountains to climb and monstrous obstacles to overcome. When the numbers are not what I want them to be, I will measure my success as I look to see the mountain behind me.*

### Set a Big Goal and Issue a Challenge

You're a business guru. You know all about goal-setting—or at least you did. Revisit this good habit by setting a measurable company goal. For example, "Our company is going to sign 20 new customers by the end of the month." Issue the challenge and break it down. Even if you miss the mark, you've created momentum. Post your company goal where all your employees can see it.

## DAY 6

> *When it is necessary, I will make big changes no matter how uncomfortable they make me feel. Transformation will not be easy, but it will be worth it.*

### Take Back Those Lost Minutes

Shatter the comfort zone by taking back the time you are losing on old habits and mundane routines.

Do you really need that coffee shop latte? Is killing 30 minutes at the water-cooler part of your plan for success?

Take a long hard look at your schedule with an eye on making some changes. Reclaim wasted time on unfruitful meetings and repetitive phone calls. Write down three things you can change and how much time you will gain back.

## DAY 7

> *My habits are important in every aspect. Even small habits will affect the big picture. I will start to develop good habits and rid myself of the bad ones.*

### Spend an Hour Each Day Meeting Potential New Clients

Introduce yourself via social media. Attend a community planning meeting. Look for ways to get involved in the community that your business calls home. This kind of momentum easily becomes progress.

Dare to reach for your dreams—again by stepping out of your comfort zone. Write down what progress might be made if you spend that hour and what you may gain from it.

# Creating Concentration

I like to think that I was born to be a leader with the full understanding of how to concentrate at any possible time, but looking back on my past, I'm afraid that's just not the case. There was a time when I was unable to step up to the plate. It took a couple of kicks in the pants, but in the end, I learned valuable lessons that have continued to help me become a better leader and a more successful person.

It may have taken a while for me to accept the fact that I was not in complete control of my life, but once I grasped that, I saw that I actually had more control over it than I had first believed. I knew this: I was a capable leader who had experienced a lot of ups and downs, and I was eager to share my ideas and to help other people rise up, too.

## DAY 1

> There will be days that I feel like I cannot
> concentrate. In those moments, I will remember
> that they are fleeting and that my focus will return.
> Frustration will only exacerbate the problem.

### It's Okay to Be Imperfect
It's a hectic and fast-paced world. With so much juggling of our time and energy on a daily basis, many of us find ourselves reaching for another cup of coffee or an energy drink to amp up our mental clarity.

I used to be afraid of my inability to be perfect. But I became more comfortable in my own skin knowing mistakes are not just normal, they are necessary. This realization, that I didn't have to be flawless, made it a lot easier for me to step up into a leadership role. I was also able to value those who served under me, seeing their mistakes as mirrors of my own. I just had to be sure that while I was leading, I could also avoid the distractions that I faced.

Take a moment to write down five things that distract you. Keep the list because we will come back to it later!

## DAY 2

> Today I will learn to be quiet. I will take
> time to listen to the world around me and
> to appreciate the sound of nothing.

### Cut Out the Noise

Many people find background noise distracting. Turning off the television and the radio can be an effective way to stay focused on the task at hand. If your brain is cluttered with outside distractions, the chance of zoning out becomes that much greater. If you can't turn off the noise, grab your headphones and put on music that calms you and lets you focus.

If you still find that you have trouble focusing, don't feel defeated. My perspective flipped. Instead of instantly feeling defeated and shutting down, I repeatedly restructured my approach until I got it right. Eventually I was able to channel my respect for imperfection into a self-perpetuating system of groundbreaking trial, acceptable error, and noticeable optimization.

Try to spend 15 minutes in silence today, whether it is at home, in the car, or at the office. Let your mind be open to the quiet. Write down the things you thought about in silence.

## DAY 3

> *There must be a feeling of contentment within my company culture. If there is a feeling of stress, I will change it. It's important to me that my employees feel relaxed and comfortable while they are working.*

### Create a Great Workspace

Organizing your space can deter chaos. You can also invest in some proper lighting and decor that you find appealing. Being comfortable while you are doing your job should be something that you do for yourself because you are worth it. When it all doesn't go the way that you want it to, don't give up!

There were plenty of times when I was more than ready to throw in the towel. After all, being a leader is a big responsibility and setbacks can be extremely frustrating—and, at first, I wasn't able to accept defeat. I got frustrated instead, losing my cool at the first sign of failure.

Do at least one thing to make your workspace feel good today. Bring in a fresh flower or a candle, or even a photo or a quote that inspires you. Use that to help you focus and motivate yourself. Write down whether you think it helped.

## DAY 4

> *I will avoid multitasking at all costs! When I let myself become distracted, the need for multitasking arises. I will focus on focusing today.*

### Limit Multitasking

Cut down on the multitasking as much as you possibly can. Try to do one thing at a time. A great way to practice this is by carrying fewer grocery bags per trip. Try to limit your multitasking at least three times today, whether it is at the workplace or at home. I learned to keep in mind that there really is a solution to everything and that every event, good or bad, has a beneficial lesson attached. By knowing these things, I was able to recollect my thoughts, find the underlying issues causing the problems, and nip them in the bud. Eventually my irritation and angst subsided, and I gained more confidence in my leadership capabilities with every solved problem.

At the end of the day, take five minutes to look over what you've done. Is your work more focused because you spent the time on only one task instead of three other things at the same time? Do you feel more clarity? Write about this experience.

## DAY 5

> *Everything doesn't happen overnight. Sometimes I simply have to take time away from it all to think about things. Today I am content with the now.*

### Take a Walk

Exercising, even just taking short five-minute walking breaks, can help ease a restless mind. Regular breaks like this are a wonderful way to brush the cobwebs out of your head. As much as I wanted it to, my success did not happen overnight. It took hard work, patience, determination, and vision—and it took a long time. I was a follower for longer than I was a leader, but I used that time wisely to gobble up as many lessons as I could.

Spend a minimum of five minutes walking today. If you can't go outside, try and walk somewhere that you haven't been before, even if it's just down a different hallway. Think about what you are seeing and not about what you are leaving behind. Write down how you felt and what you thought about.

## DAY 6

> *My brain is a computer and it needs a break sometimes.*
> *In order to be a competent leader, I need to know when it's*
> *time to stop staring at a screen and start staring at the sky.*

### Turn Off Your Devices

I know now that being a leader sometimes means taking the backseat. In fact, some of my best discoveries have been made by allowing someone else to take the reins and disconnecting for a while.

Try turning your cell phone off when you are deep at work on something that requires your entire concentration. Experiencing phantom phone ringing can cause you to become jumpy and nervous. Turning off the phone causes you less stress and helps you to keep a calmer state of mind.

I can now say, with confidence, that leadership is my calling. I know how to read people because I have been through hard times myself. I am able to stay calm in a crisis because I have learned how to sort out the details and fix the problem from the ground up. Moreover, I have humbled myself to the fact that I cannot make miracles happen instantly, and that I will have more success as a leader if I never act like a horrible boss.

Turn off your devices for at least 30 minutes today. Write down how you felt while they were off and when you turned them back on.

## DAY 7

> *I will learn from every aspect of my world. Each moment*
> *is another opportunity to learn, and I will use those*
> *opportunities to fuel my passion and create my energy.*

### Teach Yourself to Think!

Go back to the list that you made on the first day. Did we talk about some of the things that were distracting you? Can you use some of the techniques that we've discussed this week to learn to focus? How about that energy drink? Have you put it down yet?

Write down your answers and how you feel about them. Hopefully using some of these tips will help you stay clear-headed throughout your future endeavors.

I want to stress this: It is important that you teach yourself how to see the events in your life as lessons, not simply as blessings or curses. Everything—every success, every failure—has its purpose whether you can see it immediately or not. Some of the best lessons I've ever learned took a long time to come to fruition.

# *The Burnout Blues*

You hear it all the time: "Work smart, not hard."

At the same time, being a hard worker is considered a desirable trait in an individual. And when you're an entrepreneur, it's a must-have trait for success. But sometimes, working too much can lead to burnout. Instead, you should try to find ways that allow you to get both the same quality and quantity of work done, without running yourself into the ground. This week provides a few tips to help prevent burnout.

## DAY 1

> *Today I am going to breathe. I am going to focus on what it feels like to breathe and feel the energy within my body.*

### Take More Breaks

Creating a checklist of tasks may seem counterproductive, but, by allowing yourself to take several small breaks during a lengthy task, you can stay focused and allow your body to renew its energy and attention span. Use some of the techniques that we talked about last week during your break time and regain your focus.

After you take the breaks today, write down whether you felt like they helped you to stay focused.

## DAY 2

> *Organizing my world is something that*
> *is vital to my success. I'm going to focus on*
> *organizing at least one thing today!*

### Create a To-Do List

This not only keeps your mind free from cluttered thoughts but also makes you less likely to forget to finish something or meet a deadline. Try writing the list the night before. This way, you can figure out how much you need to get done, which can be helpful when scheduling your day. Plus, it can give your mind a rest. You won't be obsessing over the possibility of forgetting a task when you're trying to sleep.

Write that list!

## DAY 3

> *I know what distracts me, and I will not allow it in*
> *my world. I have a goal and I am going to reach it!*

### Create a To-Don't List

This may seem odd, but it can help you stay on task. List things like "Stay away from games" or "No phone calls." You can create a new to-don't list each day, in addition to the list of things you want to accomplish. This exercise can help keep you focused on the most important tasks in a given day and keep you from wasting time.

Create your to-don't list and implement it tomorrow.

## DAY 4

> *Just as I might track my calories or my*
> *weight, today I am going to track my progress.*
> *Every sign of change is a sign of success!*

### Keep a Pen and Paper Close at Hand

For entrepreneurs, there are many responsibilities. With those responsibilities come many things that need to be remembered. Instead of trying to keep it all in your head, jot things down on paper. Keep track of names, phone numbers, dates, deadlines, and odd jobs that need to be completed. You'll be amazed at how efficient you can be when you can refer back to written information, and your brain is no longer a cluttered mess of random thoughts.

Start jotting things down today and make a note on whether or not it helped.

## DAY 5

> *No one is going to take away my dreams! I*
> *will not allow others to destroy my energy. I*
> *will surround myself with positive people.*

### Delegate

Delegation can be hard for people who are starting their dream business. Your company is your baby. You love it, and you want everything to be perfect. But you're not a superhero, and there are others who will want your business to succeed just as much as you do.

The key is to surround yourself with and employ people who have the same vision for your business that you do. Then you can feel more comfortable with passing important duties to other hands.

Today, take one thing off your plate by delegating it to someone trustworthy within your business. Then write about how that person did handling the task without your supervision.

## DAY 6

> *Even though I want to get everything done at once,*
> *I know that I need to take my time. I won't overload*
> *myself today. I will appreciate my own time.*

### Don't Over-Schedule

When you're writing out your to-do list (and your to-don't list), try to give yourself a bit more time for a task than you think you may need. Then, in the event that you do take longer than you thought, you'll be covered. Having this buffer can also help you prepare for potential crises that tend to crop up when you're at your busiest.

Are you over-scheduled? Check out your schedule today and try and eliminate at least one thing.

## DAY 7

> *It's not always an easy thing to do, but I know that I need*
> *to rest. I will find one way to relax and rest today, avoiding*
> *all distractions and workplace matters. I matter more.*

### Rest

Choose one day each week that you will not work. There are millions of things that need to be done, but they will still be there when you get back to work. It's important to allow your body to relax and reenergize. Otherwise you may become burned out, and you may start to resent your work. Keep things positive. Take a break.

Every entrepreneur has a dream and a goal, neither of which involves anything less than an amazing product. Working smart, and not hard, is key to achieving this end.

Write down one way that you can implement a break into your schedule and go for it tomorrow.

# Harmful Habits

Isn't it time to get rid of bad habits that limit your potential? All of us develop bad habits over time. When you've been doing a particular job or been with a certain company for a while, complacency can set in. When it does, you're likely to discover some bad work habits.

Now is the time to get rid of them and develop better ones to help you become more successful.

## DAY 1

> *I cannot do this alone. I will not do this alone.*

### Stop Being a Lone Ranger

Someone who does not have a confidant at work is more likely to fail due to lack of accountability. If you have an unproductive habit that you have trouble shaking, tell someone that you can rely on. If you work with a team, let them know, if that's feasible. Then report your progress to them often. Multiple small successes soon add up to large ones.

Do you have a work confidant? Do you have a habit that you are trying to kick? Have you told your confidant?

## DAY 2

> *I know what is important to me and I will make that my priority, even when it might not seem like the most opportune time. My priorities come first.*

### Lose Your Inability to Set Priorities

If you find yourself struggling with this issue, you will soon get overwhelmed by all the demands put on you at work. Try to accomplish the larger or more difficult assignments in the morning when you are fresh and save the more repetitive ones for later in the day. If you receive assignments as the day is winding down, use the last 5 to 10 minutes to prioritize for the next day. Lists are very helpful, and checking items off as you complete them is a real ego-booster.

Prioritize tomorrow now. Make your list.

## DAY 3

> *I refuse to motivate my employees or myself in an unhealthy manner. I will find a positive way to motivate!*

### Stop Using Fear as a Prime Motivator

It's pretty easy to be motivated by fear at work. Fear of poor performance, fear of failure, fear of being a social outsider—fear will paralyze you. It will cause you to slide through the day making false starts and avoiding commitment.

The remedy for fear is planning. Start by making a list of things you have accomplished (even if it's only two or three items) and keep it in a visible place to use as self-encouragement. Then make a list of things you want to accomplish and the steps to complete each one. The best way to successfully complete a big project is to break it down into smaller pieces.

Make the list of your accomplishments now and let's start planning.

155

## DAY 4

> *I will not sit idly and let time pass me by.*
> Procrastination *is a word that will leave my*
> *vocabulary today. It no longer exists in my world.*

### Stop Procrastinating

Communication is key in the workplace. However, putting off responding to e-mails and phone calls is just kicking the can down the road. You never catch up. A large portion of correspondence is routine and doesn't need more than a "received" or a "thank you," neither of which takes very long. A quick response also helps cement good relationships with clients and coworkers.

If you think you may have some unproductive habits but aren't sure what they are, recheck your old performance evaluations from any previous job you had for patterns. Ask a trusted colleague if he or she is aware of any detrimental tendencies you may exhibit. A spouse or close friend may also be aware of potential problem areas.

When you do discover a work habit that needs changing, look for a mentor—someone who has already conquered the same problem is an ideal candidate to help you on your road to success.

Write down one work habit that you need to change and how you can do it.

## DAY 5

> *Confidence will push me forward, but*
> *arrogance will keep me from reaching my goals.*
> *I will find a balance between the two.*

### Arrogance Versus Confidence

Confidence is sometimes mistaken for arrogance in a negotiation as well as everyday life. There is a fine line between the two in spite of the fact that they are actually polar opposites. Much like a magnet with a positive pole and a negative pole, arrogance and confidence can be viewed in the same respect. Crossing that fine line or giving the appearance of crossing it can be detrimental in a negotiation or in a variety of other professional and personal situations.

Just like beauty, arrogance versus confidence is sometimes in the eye of the beholder. Someone's perception of confidence may depend on that person's cultural background. However, the key differentiator between the two is the foundation. Confidence is grounded in experience and expertise with a sense of respect and humility; arrogance is grounded in nothing (it is unwarranted, baseless confidence with a lack of respect and humility). There are varying degrees of each and it is more of a spectrum with shades of gray in the middle, but we can feel it when someone crosses the line.

Write down whether or not you feel like you are arrogant or confident and why. What can you do to make sure that you remain balanced?

## DAY 6

> *As long as I remain positive and believe in myself,*
> *I am on the right track. I will find a way to solidify*
> *my confidence and believe in my goals.*

### Arrogance Repels/Confidence Attracts

Arrogance repels positive people; it is detested in a negotiation and will hinder progress. It breaks down trust and a collaborative environment. Confidence, on the other hand, attracts positive people, fosters a collaborative environment, and promotes progress.

Sometimes it is tough to gauge how other people perceive us. If you are having trouble discerning whether you are coming across as arrogant, ask a trusted friend or business partner who has had the courage in the past to speak honestly with you about other difficult or sensitive matters.

Write down the name of the person you are going to talk to about your personality. Make sure to tell that person to be clear on why he or she believes you are arrogant or confident.

## DAY 7

> *Sincerity and honesty will get me the furthest*
> *with my employees and my customers. I*
> *will commit myself to each of them.*

### Magnetism Can Create or Destroy

Magnetism can generate electricity. It can also destroy something incredible (your computer hard drive, for instance). Likewise, confidence can create and arrogance can destroy. Unfortunately, it is much easier and quicker for arrogance to destroy than it is for confidence to create. Plus, attempting to repair what arrogance has already tarnished is very difficult.

When someone is able to carry confidence with humility in a negotiation, it is a beautiful thing. There is no doubt about that person's strength of character, purpose, passion, or resolve. Walking the fine line between confidence and arrogance is a challenge at times, but that's one of the reasons why it is so rare and precious when someone can do it.

What did your team or confidant say? Were you arrogant or confident? How did you feel about the answer?

# *Savvy Solutions*

As the person in charge of your company, you need to know how to work with people on many different levels. It is essential for leaders, especially entrepreneurs, to know how to deal with difficult people in the workplace.

An unsatisfied customer, a gossiping employee, or a know-it-all competitor—these disagreeable people are always around somewhere making our lives tougher. Becoming frustrated, stressed, and overwhelmed can hurt your business, leading to lost customers or strained relationships with employees.

## DAY 1

> *I will always give 100 percent, no matter what position I am in. I am not okay with being a deadweight.*

### The Deadweight
The deadweight is the person who doesn't carry a fair share of the workload, avoids difficult assignments, and rarely delivers on promises.

Solution: On the rare moment the deadweight does help you, be very generous with your praise. Talk with the deadweight and reinforce any positive traits that person may have, and encourage him or her to do more. Positive reinforcement can work wonders. It's a great motivator.

Write down three ways that you can implement positive reinforcement with someone who is not pulling his or her weight on your team.

## DAY 2

> *The words that come out of my mouth*
> *are just as important as my actions. I will*
> *carefully choose the things that I say.*

### The Rumor-Spreader

The rumor-spreader gossips about others and loves to spread bad news. This can be very disruptive in the workplace.

Solution: Avoid this type of person as much as possible. At every opportunity, correct distorted and untrue gossip you may encounter. Discrediting the rumor-spreader will cause people to stop listening, and without an audience to entertain, the gossip will probably halt. If you must confront someone who is maliciously spreading rumors, expect denial. Have your evidence well documented, making it impossible for that person to duck responsibility.

Write down one effective management tool when it comes to dealing with a rumor-spreader.

## DAY 3

> *I am responsible for my actions and accomplishments.*
> *It would only hurt me to take credit for something*
> *that I did not do. I will work for my rewards.*

### The Backstabber

The backstabber takes credit for your accomplishments, bad-mouths you to your employees or other important people, and says one thing to your face and another behind your back.

Solution: Of all of the kinds of difficult people, this is the one you should not tolerate, avoid, or ignore. Before confronting the backstabber, gather all of your evidence. It is important to stay calm. Present only the facts, not hearsay, innuendos, or supposition. Don't attribute motive or intent. Describe the behavior that will not be tolerated and without threats, enlighten the backstabber of the consequences if the behavior does not stop immediately.

Write down the consequences that will be used in case you do not succeed in finding a solution while having issues with a backstabber. Add those solutions to your own personal training manual.

## DAY 4

> *Without my coworkers, employees, partners, and customers, I have nothing. This company is not all about me. It takes a village.*

### The All-About-Me Person

This person cares far more about his or her own career than the good of your company and will hog the limelight at every opportunity, stepping on toes if necessary.

Solution: Confront the all-about-me person. Be direct and let that person know you will not be intimidated. If that fails, you may have to bring in a third party to act as a mediator.

Select a mediation tactic that you will use if you are in this situation and write it down. You will need these notes later.

## DAY 5

> *I don't need to be right about everything. It's okay to let others speak their minds, too.*

### The Know-It-All

The know-it-all has an inflated ego and offers unwanted advice and information to anyone who will listen. This person will be the first one to say, "I told you so" in the event you make a mistake.

Solution: Tell the know-it-all that advice has more meaning when it has been requested and not volunteered. Or you can just smile, say thank you, and ignore that person and his or her advice.

How will you tell your employees to deal with a know-it-all? Write down your advice for them.

## DAY 6

> *I refuse to complain about things that I cannot control. There is a way to find something positive in every moment and I will strive to do so.*

### The Complainer

The complainer resists change, always expects the worst, and complains about everyone and everything.

Solution: This is another person to avoid when possible. Don't get caught up in this person's negativity. Counteract each negative remark with a positive one. Write down three positive remarks that will work in a situation like this.

## DAY 7

> *My temper is something that I have control over. It's my job to stay in charge of me, and I refuse to let others break me.*

*The Firecracker*

The firecracker flies off of the handle at the slightest provocation, is highly judgmental of others, and behaves in an unprofessional manner by shouting, name calling, and even using profanity.

Solution: Let the little firecracker blow off steam. When this person cools down, respond calmly and slowly, but in an assertive way, to bring the firecracker down to your emotional level. Give this person specific feedback on explosive behavior and let him or her know that this will not be tolerated in the workplace. Videotaping the firecracker and later allowing a private viewing would be a real eye-opener.

Did you recognize anyone from this week's lesson?

Write down the names of people on your team that these profiles may personify and remember your solutions to dealing with them. These seven profiles are fairly common. They are hard to deal with and near impossible to work around. Just remember, any difficult person can be handled successfully with positive and direct communication. And then again, you could say goodbye to the difficult person on a note written on a pink slip.

# Talking Tips

Becoming a legendary orator doesn't just happen overnight. You can, however, become a great speaker if you continue to SPEAK. Influencing people with your speech is an important part of being a great leader. You must know how to effectively communicate with people and learn how to speak in a way that makes them want to follow you.

## DAY 1

> *I can say many things, but unless my actions*
> *back up my words, they are worthless.*

### Great Words Create Great Moments

*Inspiring. Confident. Humorous. Motivational. Honest. Engaging. Powerful.*

These words are used to describe great speeches. If you are preparing to give a presentation or a speech, you'll need to hone your speaking skills before that day comes. This week, follow an easy recipe for great delivery of all of your speeches. Remember to stay confident and believable when you talk to others and make eye contact as much as possible.

Today, write down some things that you feel might be holding you back with your presenting skills. Keep the list with you as you read your devotional each day and use the tips to help you with your issues. In the next five days, you will learn what the acronym SPEAK stands for, which will allow you to become a more successful presenter.

## DAY 2

> *When I am talking to someone or giving a speech,*
> *I will make sure that I can back my words up with*
> *action. I will seek out questions and give answers in*
> *a way that will help and teach at the same time.*

### The "S" in Speak Stands for Seek a Clear Direction for Your Speech

Your speech must have a focus. You won't get lost in your words if you stay moving toward your destination. That means you'll have to decide where you are going. What's the purpose? What do you want your audience to take away? Without a cohesive message, the members of your audience will be twiddling their thumbs, confused, in mid-snooze, or who knows what. Chances are that if they don't know where you're going, after a while they won't be listening to you.

Write down a format that you can follow when writing your next speech. Make sure that you include an area where you can focus on the direction of the speech.

## DAY 3

> *In order to be prepared at all times, I will be*
> *confident in my research and kind when I speak.*
> *I want to inspire future generations.*

### The "P" in Speak Stands for Prepare

Prepare, prepare, prepare. Good preparation means knowing your audience and writing your speech for the specific group you will be addressing. You've got to make sure each person in your audience can find something to which he or she can relate. Good preparation also includes knowing your subject matter inside and out. If you need to do some research, get to it. Lastly, common sense says good preparation means good practice. Good practice leads to great practice, which leads to a perfect speech.

Look up a speech that you find inspiring and recite it in front of a mirror. Be aware of your facial expressions and make sure that you are not making inconsistent faces or standing awkwardly.

## DAY 4

> *It is my job to give people hope. I want to entertain them with my words and inspire action with my thoughts.*

### The "E" in Speak Stands for Entertain

Entertain their hearts out. Good speeches often tell a story and evoke strong emotions. Many great speakers know how to successfully use humor to their advantage. Just think about your favorite comedian. That person is often mindful of who's in the audience and how to best deliver that well-planned punch line. While speeches don't always have to be chock-full of jokes, your speech should take the crowd on an exciting ride and hold everyone's attention. And if you can move your audience to tears, that speech will surely be a memorable one.

Think of three ways you can incorporate entertainment into your next speech. Use a subject that you are familiar with and may need to speak about again. Write your ideas down and save them for later.

## DAY 5

> *I cannot control my circumstances. When they are out of my control, I will relax and let things go smoothly.*

### The "A" in Speak Stands for Accept Your Circumstances

Accept the current circumstances and move on. Great speakers know how to roll with the punches. Are you speaking at a big event, at which things aren't going as planned? Is that audience a bit bigger than it was supposed to be? Did you stumble a bit over that last line?

Don't sweat it. If you act like it didn't happen, the members of your audience might not even notice. And if they do, that's life. If you are sweating, that's okay. Nerves are a part of the gig. But eventually you have to get a grip and keep going. Be strong and keep it moving.

Today write down five things that you can use to calm your nerves before and during a speech.

## DAY 6

> *When things get complicated, sometimes the best thing I can do is go back to basics. I will slow down and remember where I started and where I am going.*

### The "K" in Speak Stands for Keep It Real

So you've heard that honesty is the best policy, right? This holds true especially during a presentation. You want to stay true to yourself. If it means admitting you're nervous, that can actually work to calm you down.

Most important, you want to speak from a place where you're comfortable. And if you are pretending to be someone you're not, that's a sure-fire recipe for a speech catastrophe. Make sure that whatever you say, you stay true to your values and your message. Stay true to your voice.

What do you think that your true voice personifies? What values do you always want to be clear in the speeches that you make? Write them down.

## DAY 7

> *Every detail of my business deserves my full attention.*
> *Today I'm going to focus on the small things and make*
> *sure that I haven't missed anything along my journey.*

### Be Legendary

Becoming a legendary orator doesn't just happen overnight. But you can become a great speaker if you continue to follow the SPEAK method.

Let's take another look at that list you created. Do you think that you can overcome some of your fears by using the SPEAK method? Write down exactly what you will do to conquer your fears by learning to SPEAK. Don't stop there! Try speaking in public using these methods; see how it works and how you feel.

# *Balancing Success and Family*

By now you've spent weeks developing a laser-like focus toward your business. Your office is performing like never before, customers have never been happier, and you're beaming with a sense of pride and accomplishment. It's an amazing feeling. At the same time, however, your home life may be suffering because of your newfound dedication to business excellence.

Balancing family and success is never easy; especially when the job requires long hours at the office and/or frequent traveling. And we tell ourselves that it's the price we pay as professionals to be at the top of our game, but that's not always true. So let's spend this week getting back in touch with what really matters within our lives—the family and friends that keep us grounded and properly balanced.

## DAY 1

> *Who I am outside of my business is just as*
> *important as who I am within the business.*
> *I will focus on my personal life today.*

### The Little Things Matter
As entrepreneurs, it's far too common for us to miss out on birthday parties, dance recitals, Little League baseball games, and the little

things in life that matter so much to our family. And since we have our family's support (for the most part), we are often given a pass when we really should be attending these special events. After all, signing up a new client is more important for your success than your son's soccer game, isn't it?

Honestly, only you can answer that question . . . but I think you know how your family would respond if they were answering honestly.

So for today, your assignment is to think about your family and some of the recent activities you planned that didn't work out. Write about those things in your journal and how your family felt about you not following through on your promises.

## DAY 2

> *When my personal life has struggles, they will show up in my business. Today I'm going to focus on the people who matter to me outside of my business world and make sure they know how much I appreciate them.*

### Make Time for Quality Time

Life is short, and there is no better time than today to do something with a special person in your life. So here's your assignment: leave work after lunch and go pick up one of the people in your family that you wrote about yesterday. Then, spend a few quality hours with that person having fun . . . and do not mention a thing about work during that time. This means no cell phones, no social media, and no distractions.

Now, you're probably thinking that there is absolutely no way that you can cut out half of your day today, but figure out how to get it done. Delegate a few tasks to your assistant if necessary, or reschedule meetings for another time. The priority for the day is fun and it's long overdue.

## DAY 3

> *I will be smart about the time that I put in at work.*
> *If I work smarter I will not have to work longer.*

### Rewind and Rethink

Did you leave work early and have fun with a friend or family member yesterday? How did that make you feel?

Chances are pretty good that once you began to shift your schedule around and delegate a few of your daily tasks, the day turned out just fine. And hopefully you had a great time goofing off for a little while, but that honestly wasn't the most important task of the day. Instead, it was to make you realize that you can still have a productive workday and fun with your family as well.

Today's assignment is a simple one, but it's going to feel almost impossible at first. It's time to re-think your work schedule a little bit. Are there some tasks that you've kept that need to be delegated more frequently? Can you gain some efficiency by changing up how you communicate with customers and employees?

Do some serious soul-searching today and write in your journal about ways you can become more efficient. The goal is to find a way to balance your workweek so there's plenty of time for both work and family.

## DAY 4

> *While I have goals for my business, my purpose*
> *in life is far greater than any business will ever be.*
> *I will focus on reaching for my purpose daily.*

### Review and Recommit

Remember back in the early chapters when we talked about defining your goals and your purpose in life?

I said back then that your goals and your purpose were two completely different things. Goals are milestones that you hope to achieve in life, while your purpose is the driving force that helps get you there. And for most of us, our purpose will revolve around providing for our families.

Today, your task is to recommit to your purpose in life. Think about what truly makes you happy in life and how your family plays a part in that. Try to meditate on this idea for at least 15 minutes and write about your thoughts in your journal.

## DAY 5

> *There is great power inside of me. I want to share that power with others, and today I am going to do just that!*

### Make Dreams Come True

After spending yesterday thinking about how your family plays into your main purpose in life, now would be a good time to turn the conversation away from yourself and focus on how you can empower the people closest to you. Does someone have a dream that you can assist with? Have you even asked lately about your family's individual purposes?

After work today, spend some time with your loved ones and ask them, "How can I help you fulfill *your* dreams in life?" The answers may surprise you, so write them down in your journal and think about what you can do to help.

## DAY 6

> *I want to help other people reach their goals*
> *so that they can feel the successes that I feel.*
> *I'm going to make sure that I help one person*
> *take a step toward their goals today!*

### Take Action!

Today is a day of action.

Now that you've spoken to the people closest to you and heard about their goals in life, use your connections to help your loved ones move one step closer to their goals. The doorways you open could have life-changing consequences for those involved.

After telling your loved ones about what you've arranged for them today, write in your journal about their reactions and how those reactions made you feel. Also write yourself a note to follow up at a later time.

## DAY 7

> *Everyone needs a break. Today I am going to plan*
> *a break for myself. Small or large, I will make sure*
> *that I plan for some time with those that I love.*

### Time for a Breather

When's the last time you've had a real vacation?

I'm not talking about one of those business weekends where you're racing between conference lecturers and calling the office either. I mean a genuine vacation. White sandy beaches. Swimsuits and suntan lotion. That kind of getaway.

While your passion for success is probably one of your strongest qualities, it may also be one of your greatest weaknesses as well. Everybody needs some time to step back and recharge every now and then, and vacations have a way of refocusing us on what really matters in life outside of business.

So your task for today is to check dates with your family, hop on a vacation website, and plan an upcoming trip to get away from everything at work.

Then write a promise to yourself in your journal that you will do no work at all on this upcoming vacation. It's going to be 100 percent about you and your family.

# The Crabby Customer Conundrum

Your customers can certainly be wrong or just plain difficult, but you have to find a way to communicate with them anyway. This often means being pushed way outside of your comfort zone for something that may not necessarily be your company's fault . . . but that's what you do as a leader.

## DAY 1

> *I will embrace complaints when I receive them.*
> *A complaint is just an opportunity for me to*
> *make something better than it already was.*

### The Customer Is Always the Customer

I'm sure you are familiar with the old adage, "The customer is always right."

This sounds great, but it's not necessarily true. Your customers can certainly be wrong. What is true is that "the customer is always the customer." Even though he or she can be blatantly wrong, that person's status as your customer (and source of your livelihood) dictates that you communicate effectively with him or her.

Think of a situation in which you had to let someone be right when you absolutely thought that the person was wrong. How did it feel? What could you have done differently?

## DAY 2

> *When I make a mistake I will own it. I can be a better person if I know how to handle adversity when I face it.*

### Overcoming Obstacles

How can you overcome the anger, fear, or personality differences that lead to friction between you and your customers? This is something that everyone can LEARN.

Another adage fits this scenario: "Perception is all." One of the most common reasons for a customer to go to a competitor is his or her perception of your interactions and how that customer feels about them.

During the rest of the week, we will implement the LEARN method for dealing with difficult customers and still feeling like we've maintained our integrity. For today, make a list of some perceptions that you feel might exist about your company or even about you.

## DAY 3

> *It's possible for me to become more educated through listening, even when I am angry. I will listen when I want to lose my temper, and maybe I will learn something.*

### "L" Is for Listen

True listening seems to be a disappearing art in our culture. But in order to communicate effectively with a difficult customer, it's imperative. The ears are the only organs that deliver sound waves to the brain.

A good listener also engages the heart and mind. A good listener does not allow himself or herself to become distracted, but focuses on the speaker. This person doesn't formulate answers before the speaker completes a statement and doesn't give the appearance of being defensive.

Write down three ways that you can become a better listener.

## DAY 4

> *Finding connections with other human beings is important.*
> *I will try to be more empathetic on a daily basis.*

### "E" Is for Empathize

You can offer sympathy to a customer who is having a problem, but empathy will go much further toward achieving your goals. Put yourself in the customer's place. Wouldn't you be disgruntled, angry, and perhaps even fearful if a product or service didn't live up to your expectations? If it didn't perform according to the advertising or worse, caused some type of damage or injury?

Today, write down a memory of a time when you made a purchase that did not live up to your expectations. Remember how that felt and put the experience into words.

## DAY 5

> *When I face challenges, I will accept them. The feeling of*
> *victory is worth far more than the fear of the challenge.*

### "A" Is for Accept

Accept what the customer says at face value, even if you think the customer is wrong. Do this because that person thinks he or she is right, and perception is the most important thing.

If the customer perceives that you accept and believe him or her, that person will be more likely to relax and get to the point. A common hallmark of strained interactions is that the main bone of contention is saved for last. The complainant will build up to the real issue by talking about the peripheral ones first. And that also allows the customer to build a mountain of anger out of a molehill of frustration.

Write down one way that you can start accepting your customers with more enthusiasm.

## DAY 6

> *When I do not get respect from others, I will not be offended. I know that when a person does not show me respect it is not of my concern.*

### "R" Is for Respect

If the customer receives respect from you, he or she will likely return it. If the customer feels disrespected, it will be perceived as a personal attack. Remember, you can learn something from anybody, regardless of education level, financial situation, or physical appearance. Everyone deserves respect simply for being a human being.

Write down one customer that you are going to try and learn something from, and then reach out to this person for genuine advice.

## DAY 7

> *I will focus on resolving my differences today. I do not want conflict in my life, and I will not reach my goals if I hang on to resentment.*

### "N" Is for Negotiate

If you successfully employ listening, empathizing, accepting, and respecting, you will pave the way for negotiating. You will have put the difficult person at ease. You will have helped that person believe you are in his or her corner. That difficult person will be better prepared to drop the aggression and enter into negotiations, believing that you will treat him or her with fairness, honesty, and integrity.

Finally, always try to resolve a customer's issue with one conversation. The quicker the issue is resolved, the better the customer will feel about the interaction.

Remember that customer you were going to learn from? Did you? How did it make you feel? Did it work?

# Customers, Cash, and Commitment

You have to manage cash flow. Talking money is the key.

Perhaps the greatest hurdle for any business owner is being able to talk comfortably about money with vendors, customers, and even employees. It's a topic that sends the heart racing and creates needless stress.

## DAY 1

> *I want to make people feel good about themselves,*
> *especially my customers. I am going to give people*
> *hope for the future, one day at a time.*

### Money Matters

Are you independently wealthy? Did you start your business from lottery winnings? Or the profit from your shares of Google?

Probably not . . . so the financial health of your livelihood is at stake with every conversation you have that involves money. Every single business operates from a budget. Money pays the bills and helps your organization grow. Before your next anxiety attack, consider the three reasons revealed this week that explain why it's critical to learn how to talk about money as a business owner.

Think about a time when you were uncomfortable talking about money. What caused that feeling? What could you have done to make it better? How could talking about money have changed the situation?

## DAY 2

> *Even when profits are not high, I will remain*
> *confident in my dream and in my dedication.*

### Talking Money Shows Confidence

It's honest. And, frankly, it shows that you are confident. When the time comes to talk about pricing, instead of avoiding the issue, a successful businessperson says, "I know you're wondering what this will cost. Let me show you. . . ." How you explain depends on your business: a price range, a fee-for-service, or a breakdown of each expense.

The point here is that you should speak confidently about your pricing since your products and services are worth the expense. If you really believe that, then there is no reason to be nervous sharing it with your customers.

To help build your confidence, write in your journal today about why your pricing is actually a value to your customers.

## DAY 3

> *My ears are open and my words are chosen carefully.*
> *This day I will focus on listening to others before I speak.*

### Talking Money Shows You Have Listened

Customer satisfaction always relies on the feeling of being understood. When a customer feels "heard," he or she trusts you. And trust is the solid foundation of customer loyalty. With trust, you can educate your customer on your business and its value. The costs will easily be recognized and accepted: "Now that I understand your needs, let me explain the pricing. . . ."

Write down one new way that you can talk to your customers about costs.

## DAY 4

> *If my money is not organized I will not be able to talk about it. I will be fully educated about my finances so that I can speak freely about the subject to anyone who may ask.*

### Talking Money Is a Win-Win Situation

When discussing money with a customer, you must acknowledge that you are both seeking a positive outcome. You are looking for a sale; the customer wants a smart buy for his or her needs. When you can focus on the customer's need, you can present costs in terms of how your business will make a difference. "Based on your budget, here is what we can do to help you meet your goals. . . ."

Money is essential to your business. Learning to discuss it with clarity will improve communications with your customers and put them at ease. Don't hesitate to be honest when the topic comes up. When everyone is at ease, trust builds . . . and your business will grow as a result.

Write down a way that you can put a positive spin on an honest answer. It could be an answer that might be negative or about an expensive situation.

## DAY 5

> *If my customers are not happy, there is a reason. I will always go back to the customer and find out how to make them happy. Without their happiness, I don't have a business.*

## Know Your Customer's Name

In order to make your customers repeat buyers, building a solid relationship with them is key to cultivating loyalty and making them feel important every time that they interact with your business.

We talked about this the other week, but I'm going to say it again. Know your customer!

Make it a daily practice to learn and memorize the names of all your patrons, so they feel special the next time they return. Treat them like royalty. Lay out the proverbial red carpet every time they come in the door. Save data about your clients and build a robust digital profile about every single customer. By tracking their purchases, your support team can solve potential problems faster and in a more efficient way.

Today, write down some ideas on how you can start tracking customer purchases more efficiently and use that information to make your customers feel special.

## DAY 6

> *My feelings are important, and I will try with my utmost power to express them as needed. I want people to trust what I have to say.*

## Be Genuine

Most people can tell if someone is faking interest in them or wants to have a conversation in order to gain some type of monetary value. If customers feel like they are receiving truly genuine enthusiasm and aren't just another paycheck to you, it will benefit you in a multitude of ways. Know what your customers need and be ready to exceed their expectations.

Customers also deserve your complete attention, without interruptions. And while you may deliver that level of service every time, do your employees? If you're not sure, then working with them on these things is vital.

To help you prepare a training lesson for your employees, write down your target market's needs. Why are they coming to you as customers?

## DAY 7

*When I am doing something for a positive reason, I know that it is a good thing, no matter what the outcome is.*

### Be Proactive

You might not always know what your customers need at first. No one is a mind reader. But try your best to anticipate what they want from your business. Don't be afraid to ask what else you can do to make them happy.

Making these significant and simple efforts will give you a wealth of steadfast and loyal customers. Each positive experience that you make with a customer will reward you with more referrals, respectability, and an amazing reputation.

Come up with three different questions to ask your customers about their happiness with your service or product.

# Undo Unproductive

Wasting $30 billion a year in unproductive meetings is something that happens in business every single day . . . are you guilty? A recent study done by Atlassian showed that 31 hours a month are spent in unproductive meetings, and most employees are attending 62 meetings a month.* There are ways for you to counteract the wasted time and create a more efficient workplace.

## DAY 1

> Today I will find a way to be efficient and timely. My employees' time is just as important as my own time.

### Fast and Efficient Meetings

Meetings are a necessary part of every organization. They are where plans are made, goals are set, and reports are given. They offer the opportunity for dialogue and problem-solving, as well as the chance to get to know colleagues better. They can even make people laugh. When conducted well, meetings can help everyone be more productive. Sounds great, doesn't it?

But if your organization is like most others, meetings are a dreaded black hole, sucking time and energy from the attendees. You leave meetings feeling frustrated, wishing you could have used the time for

* https://www.atlassian.com/time-wasting-at-work-infographic

"real" work. According to Dean Newland, CEO of Mission Facilitators International, poorly run meetings also cost big bucks:

Each day, 11 million meetings take place in the United States, or 2.6 billion in a year. Based on an average salary of $30 per hour, $80 billion is spent on meetings each year in the United States. (The amount is probably higher, since most meetings involve more than two people.)

Take note of how many meetings that you have each week. Can you lower that number by communicating in different ways?

## DAY 2

> *My mission for today is all about preparation!*
> *I will not waste time by being unprepared.*

### Prepare for the Meeting

What's the purpose of your next meeting? Once you know the goals, establish an agenda. If your organization doesn't have an agenda template, this is the perfect time to implement one. List the topics, who will be presenting each one, and the time allotted for each topic.

With an agenda, you can determine who should be at the meeting. Only invite people who can move the agenda forward. If there are materials for a topic, they should be distributed two days prior. People should come to the meeting prepared to make the most of their time together.

Write down a list of things that your employees need to understand in order to come to every meeting prepared.

## DAY 3

> *I will not be afraid to talk about things that make*
> *me uncomfortable. Today, anything is on the table!*

## Use the Meeting to Promote Discussion and Make Decisions

You may be surprised—and pleased—to know that I discourage the use of PowerPoint presentations during meetings; it slows the pace and can be distracting. A single slide or two of data for visual purpose is fine, but no more endless, boring presentations.

By establishing a time frame for each agenda item, you can keep discussions going and redirect attention as necessary. You may even want to try a stand-up meeting! People are energized and focused; rambling sidebar conversations disappear. Assign ownership to action items, as well as deadlines. By the end of the meeting, there should be no "orphan items" without someone responsible for completing them and reporting back to the group.

Make a list of action items for your next meeting and be specific.

## DAY 4

*Today I will take action and inspire
other people to do the same.*

## Send the List of Action Items (and Deadlines) Again After Each Meeting

Although everyone should leave the meeting on time and be clear about their responsibilities, your follow-up e-mail will serve as a reminder. Rather than wait until the next meeting, people can send their reports to others by e-mail. This prevents the same agenda items from appearing again and again at future meetings.

Learning how to run an effective meeting can change your organization, increase job satisfaction, and actually boost productivity. Now that sounds better, doesn't it?

What positive things can you include in the list that will help encourage your team?

## DAY 5

> *I know what my strengths are and I am going to use them to keep my company culture alive.*

### Know Your Strengths

If you want to run a successful business, then you have to know how to play to your strengths.

It's pretty easy to micromanage everything. You may think that you can get tasks done better and more efficiently than anyone else. That might even be true, but all the time you are spending doing jobs that other people could be doing is time that you are not running your business. When you get bogged down in simple details that your employees could be working on, you are not being an effective leader.

As the leader of your business, you are responsible for spotting problems and delegating solutions. You are responsible for setting goals and thinking about the future. The only person in your company who will be genuinely motivated to grow your company is you. Every minute that you spend working on tasks that can be delegated is a minute that you are not planning, strategizing, and building the best business possible.

Now, write down the names of three people whom you trust to delegate jobs to that you are doing. Remember that you can't keep your employees from being unproductive if you are part of the problem . . . so free yourself up by deciding on those you can really trust.

## DAY 6

> *I will make it a point today to make sure that my employees know that I respect them as human beings, not just as employees. They need to know that they matter.*

### The Big Picture

It's important to work on your business not in your business. You are in charge of the big picture. When you see areas that need improvement, delegate the work so you can continue to be the troubleshooter and visionary that you need to be. It may take some practice if you're used to being really hands-on in your business, but your employees will appreciate the trust and responsibility you give them. You will quickly learn that you can do the job of leading your business that no one else can do!

Yesterday you wrote down three people whom you trust. Now write down the three jobs that you will delegate to them and implement that plan tomorrow. You can do this!

## DAY 7

> *I will continue to allow my employees to be more productive. By showing them trust, they will trust me more and we will be more successful as a team.*

### Full Circle

Do you realize what you did in the past two days? By delegating those jobs out, you've made yourself and your employees more productive. You have more time on your hands, and now they want to strive to be better and do better because you've proven that you have faith in them!

The term "delegate" embraces much more depth and human connection than its present usage. It means to trust, commit, and even depend on. Intellect modifies the action and emotion complements it. In other words, mental planning is the father of delegation details while our heart motivates.

Write down how you emphasized one employee's strengths by delegating a job to him or her. How did it make you feel?

# The Networking Novice

Effective networking is critical to growing a successful business. Networking, which is the act of making and using contacts, helps you create a pool of people who can help you and whom you can help. When people network with each other and share their expertise and skills with you, they help you improve your position as a job-seeker or businessperson. Thus, networking is certainly an effective business tool.

But how do you network effectively? This week will focus on ways to grow your networking skills.

## DAY 1

> *My vision can change the world. My community, my office, and my company are all part of my vision and through each one, I can make a difference.*

### Remember That Networking Is a Two-Way Street

It's important to remember that networking is always a two-way street. Whenever someone asks you about your service, product, or business, be sure you ask them about theirs as well. You can start from the basics: What company do they own or work for? How are they affiliated with it? Who are their clients?

Once you know the basic facts about your businesses, find out how you both can benefit each other. Write down some of the questions that you need to learn about networking.

## DAY 2

> *Fraternizing with my competition or other people within my field is important. It's not always easy to share ideas, but it is important. Today I will let go of some control.*

### Understand the Business of Those in Your Network

It's worth your time to understand the business of those in your network. What do they do? Who are the people they do it for? What other people do they collaborate with? Likewise, it is important that they understand what you do as well. This being said, it's a good sign if they're asking you as many questions about your business as you're asking them about theirs.

What questions do you have for other businesses in your network? Make a list of questions to keep handy.

## DAY 3

> *I will not disregard anyone today. Even the smallest connection may prove to be vital somewhere down the line.*

### Prioritize Your Network

It's always a good idea to evaluate the value of the contact. You want to prioritize your contacts and get in touch most often with those who will be most useful to you.

This being said, after meeting someone, ask yourself if that person is worth meeting again and if you can build a mutually beneficial relationship. How can you both help each other? Furthermore, you want to ask yourself if that person's network will be of use to you in the future. Both parties can benefit not only from each other's services but also from each other's networks.

## DAY 4

> *Even when I feel wronged, I must try to forgive.*
> *Holding in anger causes stress and keeping*
> *things copasetic is a good business move. Today*
> *I will try not to take things personally.*

### Don't Burn Bridges

Try your best not to burn bridges. You never know when someone might be able to help you in some way. Even if you think someone is not useful to you right now, that person might be useful to you in the future.

Come up with five solutions that can get you through a situation where you may want to burn a bridge with someone. Be clear and specific in the ways that you can maintain a copasetic relationship with the person or with the company.

## DAY 5

> *When I come up with new ideas, I will go*
> *after them immediately. If not now, when?*

### Marketing Your Company

Successfully marketing a new company is one of the most difficult parts about starting a business. You're done with your new business plan and your products and services are ready to be launched. The big question now is: How do you get others to know about your startup?

With so many startups around these days, standing out can be tough. However, there are several ways to make sure your startup reaches a receptive audience.

Write down some ways that you may have already tried to market your startup and let's see if they coincide with our tips over the next two days. If not, you can align them at the end of the week.

## DAY 6

> *Everyone may not like my idea. Lots of people may reject it! Eventually, someone will love it. I will stay confident.*

### Submit Your Startup to Directories

One way to market your startup is to submit it to directories like Go2Web20 and Crunchbase. Some of them are free, but others require payment. Getting your startup listed in these directories will give your website more traffic and help other businesses find out about you. For more directory help, marketer David Gray's website provides a list of more than 100 free ones you can start with (http://iamdavidgray.com/101-online-business-directories-for-local-marketing).

Getting listed on websites that group similar websites together, such as SitesLike, is another way to get others talking about your startup. Get yourself listed on at least one of these sites today!

## DAY 7

> *My company is worth more than anyone will ever realize. I am not afraid to tell anyone and everyone about it. I will dare to be brilliant every second of the day and good things will happen.*

### Get in Touch with Media Editors and Industry Bloggers

One way to get the word out about your startup is to pitch your story to news editors, industry bloggers, and startup magazines. Let's call these people influencers. They have access to wide audiences and can influence public opinions on industry trends, products, and even companies. Write them a few short paragraphs about who you are, what your startup does, and, on a bigger scale, what problems your product or service solves.

Besides pitching, another way to make an impression on media editors and industry bloggers is to send them free products or special deals in exchange for a review. You can also ask them if they're interested in an affiliate marketing partnership, where they will receive commission every time someone clicks on a link to your product and/or purchases it.

What's more, it's always a good idea to find out if influential editors and bloggers are looking for guest posts for their news websites or blogs. If so, come up with two or three good topics for a post and pitch the idea to them. Write down those topics and think about your pitch for them.

# Loyalty and Livelihood

A loyal customer base is the number one goal of most business owners. So how do you build that loyalty?

## DAY 1

> *It only takes one loyal customer to start to build my empire. I will find that one today.*

### Win Them Over with Service

A loyal customer is the number one goal of most business owners. With so many competitors on the market, entrepreneurs must do something to stand out from the crowd. More than that though, they must have customers fall in love with their businesses. What can you do to make customers love you and become diehard fans?

With customer service waning, a little bit of friendly service goes a long way. Give customers great service and you have a customer for life. Zappos did this with their free returns policy and amazing customer service, and it helped them to grow into the company they are today. Treat customers like royalty the second they walk in the door or when talking to them on the phone. Go above and beyond every time.

Write down one area where you think that your service excels. Brag a little!

## DAY 2

> *I am not afraid to put myself out there. I will work as hard as I have to in order to seize every opportunity.*

### Become an Integral Part of Your Customer's Lifestyle

When you fit a customer's life so perfectly, the customer can't imagine living without you. Brands like Whole Foods or Natural Grocers give their customers access to healthy, organic food that fits their eco-conscious lifestyle. Learn what your customers want and if you can provide it; then do it.

Do some research on a company or two that you haven't connected with yet, even though they are an ideal customer that would love your products or services. How can you make them need you?

## DAY 3

> *I am building my company because I love it.*
> *The money and success will come later.*

### Make Them Feel Like Insiders

When you know a secret before others, you feel good about yourself. It proves that you're a person worthy of an inside deal. Membership-based companies such as Costco and Sam's Club use this method to get customers coming back for more. Give them special deals for signing up for your mailing list or on social media. Tell them about a deal when they walk in the door.

Write down some ways that you can start making your clients feel like you are letting them in on a big secret. Use the tactic at least once this week.

## DAY 4

> *My reputation matters. I will strive to uphold a*
> *reputation that is associated with honesty, integrity, and an*
> *outstanding product or service. Nothing else will suffice.*

### Give Them the "Coolness" Factor

Companies like Virgin America or Warby Parker carry a lot of social clout for their customers. People who buy from these types of companies get bragging rights and that goes a long way.

Your job as an entrepreneur is to create a product that falls into that same "must have" level. You can use influencers and brand ambassadors in your community to help you make that happen.

However you go about doing it, making lasting customers is all about creating an emotional attachment. Get your customers to fall in love with your business and you have loyal users for life and more raving fans than you know how to handle.

How can you create an emotional attachment with your customers? What efforts will you need to put forth? If you're not sure of the right answer, then it's time to find it quickly.

Write your discoveries down in your journal.

## DAY 5

> *I am worthy and deserve more than I ask*
> *for. I will work for what I deserve and when*
> *it comes, I will reap the benefits.*

### Know Your Worth and Your Employees' Worth

A basic rule in life is that if you don't ask for more, you're not going to get more.

Everyone wants to move up the ladder at work, whether you're at an entry-level position or you've already been working for many years.

However, it is possible to get stuck at a certain level in terms of what you do as well as your salary.

If you're going to try to negotiate on your own behalf or with an employee, you need to first know the actual worth of every position. This means doing some research. You can look at job listings in your field, note what type of qualifications they're looking for, and how much they're willing to pay. You can also get in touch with friends working in the same field and find out how much they're making. If you're willing to go even further, contact a head hunter and find out what salary level they would be willing to send you (or your employee) on interviews for.

Complete that research today and write your true worth in your journal. Or if an employee has approached you for a raise recently, complete the research on them instead.

## DAY 6

> *I want to do everything. I know I can, but I cannot do everything all at once. I will manage my time today.*

### Watch Your Timing

If you find out that you're worth a lot more than you're getting right now, then it may be tempting to contact your clients and start making demands. That's probably a bad move, though. Putting pressure on the backbone of your company is risky.

Don't wait until you feel that your clients are taking you for granted. It helps if you reach out to them when things are going well—when you've just landed a big account or the company in general is making a lot of money. If you time your appointment badly, such as when the market is down or the company is not at the top of their game, you will definitely have some problems.

Sometimes, it helps to take advantage of opportunities that present themselves unexpectedly. For example, if you're in a meeting with a client and the two of you receive some good news, go ahead and talk about raising your prices, even if you hadn't meant to do so. *Carpe diem!*

Write down the things that you'd like to talk to your clients about—both financially and otherwise. Now prioritize the list and think about how you can start those conversations.

## DAY 7

> *Whatever it takes, I will get noticed. I will not sit back*
> *and wait for success to find me. I will find success.*

### Get Noticed

You may be the kind of person who prefers to keep your head down and go about your business. Unfortunately, that's the kind of person who doesn't always get the recognition he or she deserves. You need to start speaking up and getting noticed if you want to get that client or sell yourself to a company that might want to use your ideas. If you're just going in for a meeting, you need to speak confidently. This means that you need to be confident.

After all, confidence can only be faked for so long. You may be able to do it in the initial interview, but if you can't keep up the charade, the higher-ups are going to take notice. So do a bit of soul-searching. If you feel that you lack confidence, you need to ask yourself why this is the case. Do you truly have a weakness that you're trying to hide or are you simply an anxious person who can't stop thinking about the worst-case scenario? Take action to resolve these issues and you'll find yourself becoming more confident and getting the recognition you deserve.

How do you feel about your confidence level? What can you do about it?

# Sticky Situation Solvers

When you're the boss and everyone is counting on you to stay calm and make good decisions, what do you do? It's tough being in the center of so many sticky situations.

This week, let's figure out some ways to get unstuck.

## DAY 1

> *When a problem arises, I will solve it without question.*
> *It's not where the problem came from that matters; it's how*
> *efficiently it was solved that makes all of the difference.*

### "Houston, We Have a Problem!"

This famous sentence is one of the best illustrations of a large and looming crisis.

However, when *you* are the boss, there may be no Houston to call, no team of scientists burning up the keyboards looking for a solution. No secret computers to query and run scenarios with.

Nope. It's all down to you. It's Leadership 101 (or 102, depending on the dilemma) and the course is Problem-Solving: What to Do When Everything Goes Wrong. Will you pass or fail?

When the big "uh-oh" manifests in the workplace, don't go into defensive mode and make a bunch of whimsical decisions. As a matter of fact, stop making decisions until you get all the facts. Many times, snafus are much smaller than they first appear but an overreaction can make them worse. So stop the presses and gather the facts.

Truthfully, during the initial stages of problem-solving, your first response is rarely the best one. One of the best first steps to solving a problem is reserving judgment until all the facts are analyzed.

How have you overreacted to a problem in the past? What could you have done differently?

## DAY 2

*Once a problem is solved, I will then focus on preventing it from happening again without crushing anyone's spirit.*

### Learn from the Problem

We've all heard it said, "You learn from your mistakes, not your successes."

Why? Because problems force us to take a look at what went wrong. There's no better time to learn than when you are looking for a solution. Embrace the opportunity; it could turn out to be a blessing in disguise later on down the road. So you examine the timeline and figure out where the hamster fell off the wheel.

However, a good leader won't focus strictly on fault-finding; a good leader looks for answers instead of someone to blame. Corrective behavior may come later, but not during this stage of problem-solving.

What can you do to encourage an employee who is at fault? How can you create a winning situation from a difficult one? Make note of it!

## DAY 3

*I will be steadfast in my convictions. My strength is what has gotten me this far, and I am not giving up any time soon.*

### Be Honest with Clients

You knew it would be a tight turnaround, but now your whole line of production has gone wrong and you can't deliver to customers as promised. What do you do?

You have to be honest with those who depend on you. Just hoping things get fixed in time to deliver on a deadline isn't good leadership. Be frank but optimistic about where your company stands with the people who need to know. Having a reputation of integrity and honesty is far better than a reputation of making a few mistakes along the way.

Survey some of your employees and find out exactly what they think of the company and where your reputation stands. Be clear that honesty will not be disciplined and keep an open mind.

## DAY 4

> *When things do not go as planned, I will be honest and open with my staff. Sugarcoating will only make things worse.*

### How to Talk to Your Employees About Difficult Things

Let's take what we learned yesterday and apply it to our employees. What do you do if you made a promise to your staff and you can't deliver? For example, what if you can't afford to give company bonus checks on time?

Just like with your customers, honesty is still the best policy . . . to an extent. So face the problem head-on and give a clear explanation of any setbacks, but pay careful attention to avoid giving employees a reason to panic. As we've touched on several times in other chapters, your confidence will determine whether the setback is a minor issue or a catastrophic one.

Is there something that you need to tell your employees that you've been putting off? Write in your journal how you can deliver the news in a clear, concise matter that instills confidence in your leadership abilities.

## DAY 5

> *I will ask my employees what they need from me and how I can make their jobs better. Their feedback may not always be what I want to hear, but I promise to listen.*

### Feedback Matters

Do you actively seek feedback from your employees, your customers, and even complete strangers?

It's always great to hear when your company is doing a good job, but a true leader will work even harder to obtain the more critical feedback that we don't necessarily want to hear. It is difficult to hear about lapses in customer service, improvements that may be needed in marketing or delivery, or improvements that are necessary in production and service. When you tackle these problems efficiently and successfully, you will develop a reputation and people will want to work with your company. Thanks to gaining feedback, you are able to fix the issues and make them positive parts of your business. A reputation of reliability when it comes to these issues is something that can make or break a popular global brand.

Think about the last time a customer or an employee came to you with a scathing complaint. Did you take this feedback to heart? Are there ways you can encourage people to give more of this type of feedback?

Ponder these things throughout the day and write your solutions down in your journal.

## DAY 6

> *When I feel betrayed or let down, I will not seek retribution. I will use my power to fix the problem and move on.*

## Think About Different Solutions

Let's look at the other side of the coin for a moment and think about a time when someone you depended on did something that could have harmed your business. For example, let's say your ad agency missed a critical campaign window and now your warehouses are overflowing with unsold product because of it. What's the best way to handle this situation?

Remember what we learned the other week about assessing problems? Your first reaction is probably not going to be the best way forward. So before you pick up the phone and explode on someone, take a few deep breaths and let yourself calm down. Then focus on finding a solution that will get you out of the current predicament—whether it's through the person or company that made the mistake or another path entirely.

Now, grab your journal and write about a time when you could have handled a situation better with a vendor or any outside agency. Then jot down a few notes on how you can better deal with these issues in the future.

## DAY 7

> *Communication is vital to my business. I will keep the lines of communication with my employees and customers free and open at all times.*

## Keep the Lines of Communication Open

Do you properly keep your customers "in the loop" on the evolution of your company?

Fewer and fewer businesses seem to actively open channels of two-way communication these days, even though that's exactly what most consumers are seeking on the Internet. Something as simple as an occasional blog or social media post can help you remain relevant in the eyes of consumers, even if they are not actively making purchases from you.

Why does this matter? Well, let's say your team handles a customer's needs badly. If that client feels attached to your culture, then he or she is far more likely to give you the opportunity to make things right. On the other hand, if the client hasn't heard anything from your business for months and the mistake happens, then there is little incentive to stick around once a mistake happens.

Your assignment for today is to write a blog post and share it with the world. Tell everyone about the exciting things happening behind the scenes with your company and what they can expect in the months to come.

# No, No, No

Being able to say no is an important skill for all entrepreneurs to have. When you say no, you are really saying yes to something else. That something can be what keeps your business healthy and on track.

## DAY 1

> *My need to be liked will not outweigh*
> *my need to be successful.*

### Please Like Me!

Everyone wants to be liked. It doesn't matter if you are in third grade, on a first date, or running a business, you want to feel appreciated and respected. You want to build a relationship within the community. In each of these situations, you're willing to do a few things to succeed: pay for dinner at a great restaurant, sponsor your best friend's kids' Little League team, or buy that advertising campaign you know will not work.

Can you think of a time that you said yes when you should have said no? What was the situation? Why did you give in?

**DAY 2**

> *When the time comes to say no, I will do it in*
> *a way that is open and clear. It isn't always easy,*
> *but saying yes to everything is impossible.*

### Say "NO" to Requests That Don't Benefit You

Are you willing to say no? Refusing a request, even when done well, can feel like a poor business decision. You worry that you have alienated a customer or that you are passing up an interesting opportunity.

If it doesn't fit with your company's vision and values, then just look away. You know what you're good at and how you see the future. If an offer or idea doesn't quite align with your plans, then you should not have a problem saying no.

Have you allowed a request that didn't coincide with your goals? Did it affect you? How about your company?

**DAY 3**

> *No matter how great the achievement is, I will not*
> *be satisfied. My future is still being determined.*

### Say "NO" to Overspending

If it costs more than you can afford, then always say no. This seems obvious, but it can be hard to do when you're trying to expand your business.

You'll want to take chances and try new ideas, so keeping your focus can be challenging. You may think to yourself, "But what if that sales rep is right? Would it be so bad to go into a little debt for a few months?" Yes, it would be—stick to your budget, make money, and bank it.

Write down some ways that your budget has been busted because of not saying no. Think about how it affected your company. Was it really worth saying yes?

## DAY 4

> *When people consistently let me down, I will*
> *know that it is time to walk away. I will learn*
> *to say no to those who do not support me.*

### Say "NO" to Enablers

Say no to people who don't support you. If you decided to lose 30 pounds, you wouldn't want to be around anyone who was always offering you cake, or telling you that you'd never drop that much weight. The same goes for people who can't seem to get behind you. They can drain your soul and make you feel bad. Stick with folks who can cheer you on and celebrate your successes, big and small.

Today, say no to someone who is always bringing negative energy and write down how it made you feel.

## DAY 5

> *I cannot do it all.*

### Say "NO" to Doing It All

No one can handle everything in a business. If you're a software genius, chances are you're a terrible accountant. If you're an accountant, you are probably lousy at creating logos. When you can admit that you lack a business skill, say no to trying to do it anyway. You will save time and money by hiring someone to take on the task.

Write down your goals for saying no to people you really like. Keep those notes nearby so that you can rely on them if you start to feel the need to say yes. Just don't do it! No!

## DAY 6

*Even on the worst days and in the worst moments,*
*I refuse to give up. Nothing can stop me.*

### Say "NO" to Rushed Decision-Making

Decide how your business will handle situations like last-minute or urgent requests, charity donations, or invitations to sponsor a soccer team. Deciding ahead of time what will give you the best return on your investment can make it easier to say no. Be persistent in your goal to say no in order to help your business. Remind yourself by making a note of the positive things that will come from simply saying no.

Today, meditate over things you should have said no to long ago and envision what separating those things from your life will do for you.

## DAY 7

*My life is better now that I have learned to say no to*
*things that I cannot handle. I will say no more often.*

### Just Say "NO"

Saying no is an important business tool and key to success. You are in good company when you learn to decline requests. Make a list today of seven things that you can start saying no to now that you've learned some new tricks. Hold yourself accountable to those things and don't give in. It may be hard at first, but in the long run, it will help you and your business succeed. If you feel the urge to give in, go back to the list and remember why you need to say no. Don't give in!

Write down three different ways that you can say no without being offensive.

# Consistent Improvement

Being self-motivated is a trait that very few can confidently say they have. This is largely because as humans, we often try to make a massive change once we realize something isn't right. When you become aware of a habit or bad behavior that needs to be changed, the mind has a way of overreacting and trying to change it using the "cold turkey" approach. In actuality, this strategy makes most people feel overwhelmed and frustrated with the sheer magnitude of energy that it takes to accomplish these changes. As a result, we often fail.

## DAY 1

> *My energy is important and I will use it wisely.*

### Use the Force

As a living being, our body carries a great deal of energy and force that can be projected to the world and used in instrumental ways. This energy is largely consumed by our brain and organs, in order to keep bodily processes moving and ensure we stay alive. However, if you have ever experienced the fight-or-flight response, you are familiar with the fact that we have an overwhelming amount of energy available to us at any given time.

What struggles do you face as an entrepreneur? How have you dealt with them? Make a list of the things you think you struggle with most as an entrepreneur and how you feel that you can fix them.

## DAY 2

> *When something seems to be sucking up all of my energy and time, I will take a step back and reevaluate the situation. Maybe there is something I need to change.*

### Invest Energy Wisely

When you start to picture your body as an energy source, you realize that investing too much energy into any one given task is a major misuse. Rather, making consistent and incremental improvements will harness this energy in the correct way and allow you to take a calm and rational approach to changing your habits.

Let's use Human Resources as an example. Most likely, your business isn't going to be big enough to have a full-fledged HR department in the beginning, so you will be the one who will have to hire and fire people. As for the ones who become a part of your company, you'll need to make sure that they stay motivated and satisfied.

How can you create a plan to motivate your employees on your own? What can you do to ensure that you are creating a company culture that you are proud of? Write a mission statement in your journal that lays out exactly what you want your company culture to be like. Then create three ways you can motivate potential employees through that culture.

## DAY 3

> *Changing things up all at once may scare some of my employees and customers and be stressful for me. I will change things a little bit at a time.*

### Focus on Change

Focusing on change in increments is ideal because it consumes much less energy. Being consistent with daily improvement takes a small amount of daily energy. On the contrary, trying to make a massive change in one day will consume your body's energy entirely and leave little for the following days.

People don't usually see themselves as culpable. Maybe this is something that's written into our DNA, or maybe it's just the way that we've evolved. But the truth is that human beings generally think that they're good, even if they aren't.

Do you have an employee who is rotten, but he or she doesn't seem to realize it? How can you more effectively manage that employee? Write down some ideas.

## DAY 4

> *If I notice that my habits are inhibiting me, I will try to change them. I will not let a bad habit kill my momentum.*

### Get Rid of Negative Habits

Negative habits only become extremely taxing on the body when they form an addiction or misuse. This is true for playing video games, watching excessive television, or anything else. If these habits were done in moderation, there wouldn't be such a significant need to change them.

This holds true for positive habits as well. If you were balanced and consistent in your efforts to form positive habits, it would be much easier for you to accomplish your goals. By trying to make massive change, you are disrupting the balance in your life and that will make it harder to be consistent.

Do you know someone who tries to help but fails consistently? How can you help that person learn that what he or she is doing isn't quite right without overstepping any boundaries?

**DAY 5**

> *When people do not accept the changes I present*
> *them with, I will find a way to help them realize that*
> *I am on their side. I will not place any blame.*

## Implementing Change

As you are trying to implement change, it won't be easy.

If an employee is taking 20-minute breaks every time he or she is offered a 10-minute break, that person is pushing you. Maybe that person is spending half of the day on social media. Encouraging such an employee to change without creating drama is difficult. Most people will likely defend the things they have done. They're not readily going to admit to being the culpable party. They'll find reasons to justify why they did what they did. You might call it rationalization, but, as Sigmund Freud pointed out, rationalization is an important defense mechanism that human beings have developed in order to keep going.

How can you combat rationalization? Write down two ways.

**DAY 6**

> *My words will come from a place of kindness at all times.*

## Know When to Compromise

The next time you're tempted to pour on the blame when it comes to one of your employees, take a minute to see it from his or her point of view. You may still think that what the employee did was wrong, but if you see it with his or her rationalizations in mind, you'll realize that the person had a reason for doing it. It might not have been a good reason, but there was a rationalization. Rather than criticizing the employee, it's a good idea to address the issue in a positive way.

Make a list of some things that you can do to help an employee learn from his or her mistakes. Try to use it when you are placed in a situation like the ones that we've talked about this week.

**DAY 7**

> *I will learn to balance my power in*
> *a way that helps everyone.*

## With Great Power Comes Great Responsibility

As the boss, you have a great deal of power. And depending on your management style, you may or may not use that power effectively to keep your company running like a well-oiled machine.

Some bosses are too soft and their employees walk all over them; others are always in a rage and not putting up with any slackers. But neither of these styles brings out the best in your workers, and your job as the boss is to find a happy medium.

So toughen up . . . or relax a little bit. To be successful, think about how consistency, balance, and moderation can be integrated into your life to promote meaningful change. The power of consistent incremental improvement over massive change is so significant that when you start focusing on this transformation, it will become apparent to you that this is the only way to move forward with your life and accomplish your goals.

# Negotiating Knowledge

Learning to negotiate is one of the most important business skills you can have.

"What's your best price?"
"That's way too expensive."
"Your competitor is selling the same thing for $X."

Most salespeople and business owners hear statements like that every day. People expect to be able to negotiate, which means that you need to be prepared to answer those questions quickly, efficiently, and in a way that will promote your business.

## DAY 1

> *The art of compromise is something that I will perfect. I can negotiate through any situation.*

### Learn to Flinch

The flinch is one of the oldest negotiation tactics around. It's a visible reaction to an offer or a price, and the objective of this negotiation tactic is to make other people feel uncomfortable about the offer they presented. Here is an example of how it works.

A supplier quotes a price for a specific service. Flinching means that you respond by exclaiming, "You want how much!?!" The shock and surprise should visibly show on your face, even if you happen to think the offer is pretty fair. Unless the other person is a well-seasoned negotiator, he or she will likely become uncomfortable and/or concede to a lower price.

Your task today is to make someone flinch. If you're not ready to try in a business sense yet, then try it out on a friend or family member. Then write about how it felt to use this tactic.

## DAY 2

> *I will do my research. If I know the facts, I will be able to answer questions from an informed standpoint.*

### Know Your Stuff

Remember that the person with the most information usually does better.

When approaching a business deal, you need to learn as much as possible about the other person's situation. This is a particularly important negotiation tactic for salespeople, so ask your prospect questions about why he or she wants to make a purchase. Learning this person's wants and needs can give you an advantage. Develop the habit of asking questions such as:

"What prompted you to consider a purchase of this nature?"
"Who else have you been speaking to? How did that work out?"
"What time frames are you working with?"
"What is most important about this purchase to you?"

The basic rule is that if you don't ask for more, you're not going to get more.

So today, write your own list of questions that should be asked of every customer to better qualify each one's needs.

## DAY 3

*I am going to go to bed happy tonight.*

### Negotiate and Know What You Have to Offer

You can also apply negotiation tactics to things other than sales.

Say, for example, that you are seeking an introduction to someone who's a great fit for your company as an employee or a customer. It may feel awkward at first asking an acquaintance to help your business for nothing in return, but it doesn't have to be a one-sided benefit if you paid attention to yesterday's assignment.

Everyone needs something. Figure out what you have to offer to others in order to make your goals align.

Write down some of the connections you may want to work with and make it a point to contact them as soon as you can.

## DAY 4

*I will never miss an opportunity to try. Even when it seems impossible, I will give it a shot.*

### Go For It

Sometimes you just have to go for it.

Maybe you don't have enough information or the right contacts to make something happen, but that shouldn't stop you from giving it the old college try anyway. Salespeople generate billions of dollars of revenue every year by cold calling potential customers, and you need to have this type of confidence in your negotiating skills.

Today, reach out to someone who could be an incredible asset to your business . . . even if you do not know the person personally. Then write about the experience in your journal, regardless of whether your attempt was successful or not.

## DAY 5

> *I will utilize my thoughts today. In order to reach my goals, I must focus on the prize! I will be relentless in my negotiations.*

### The Art of Reflection

How did the little experiment go yesterday? Was reaching out to that person you had your eye on a success?

Here's a little secret—one of two things happened. Either you met your objective and you were incredibly successful, or the person blew you off... and you were still successful. Because mastering the art of negotiation is just like learning to ride a bicycle; success comes from the actual repetition.

Today your assignment is simple; just reflect on how the conversation went yesterday and think about what you could have done differently to make the outcome even more positive. Then write your ideas in your journal.

## DAY 6

> *My confidence is the key to my success.*

### Practice at Every Opportunity

Most people hesitate to negotiate because they lack the confidence. So develop this confidence by negotiating more frequently. Ask for discounts from your suppliers. Ask for a price break when you are buying from a retail store. Little things like this get you into the negotiating mindset.

Just remember to be pleasant and persistent but not too demanding. Conditioning yourself to negotiate at every opportunity will help you become more comfortable, confident, and successful.

Write down four different ways that you can negotiate. These could be in passing or during a conversation with a customer. How can you throw in a negotiation tactic without being obvious?

## DAY 7

> *When it is time, I will walk away from a situation that is not healthy. I refuse to put my body or mind through unnecessary stress.*

### Maintain Your Walk-Away Power

I learned this from a Peace Corps volunteer in my first weeks as a volunteer in Central Asia. He would have cash in his hand and very visible to the vendor around; then he would make an offer on an item. But if he did not get his price, he would just walk away. Almost every time, the vendor chased after us.

It is better to walk away from a sale than give too much of a concession by overpaying. One thing I have learned in building my business is that everything is negotiable—you just have to ask.

Today, think about your business purchases and things that you may be overpaying for. If one thing really stands out, contact that vendor and threaten to walk away. Or if you're not sure, then reach out to a new vendor and try the same approach.

# The Creativity Culture

Being creative is something that isn't always associated with business, but it should be. In order to stand out as an entrepreneur and in business, you've got to have something that makes you or your company special. When Google implemented a flexible schedule and video games in the workplace, people thought they were nuts. However, it's created a culture of creativity within the workplace. When you think outside of the box and are creative and innovative, you are headed toward all sorts of successful endeavors.

## DAY 1

> No matter how much I know, that knowledge will
> never be more powerful than my imagination.

### Knowledge Is Limited and Imagination Is More Important

Take a moment to consider that statement: Knowledge is limited and imagination is more important. This statement is counter to what most people are taught in school and the way many companies operate. "Knowledge is power" is the more common sentiment, by far.

But the ability to imagine is innate. Kids use imagination to invent games and stories that guide their play. Even adults who claim not to be particularly imaginative can picture themselves sitting down to a favorite meal or getting a promotion. Lack of imagination isn't the problem. The unwillingness to express what's imagined is.

The kind of imagination that leads to innovation carries a degree of risk. This is particularly true if a business doesn't actively support creative (aka disruptive) thinking. There is the risk of being wrong or ridiculed. There's also the risk that no one else will listen or understand.

Try to imagine something you would like to try but the risk has stopped you. Write down what might have happened if it had worked.

## DAY 2

> *I will share my love of innovation with others. In order to become successful, I need to successfully train other people to be innovative like me.*

### Imagination Creates Innovation

Businesses that foster true innovation have a culture that encourages imagination and free expression. According to an article in the *MIT Sloan Management Review*, researchers studied 759 companies in 17 major markets and concluded that, "Corporate culture was a much more important driver of radical innovation than labor, capital, government or national culture."* They also identified characteristics that innovative corporate cultures share: investment in learning and creativity.

Values are reflected in how a company spends its money. Truly innovative companies invest heavily in continuous learning and activities that promote creativity and entrepreneurial thinking.

What kinds of activities can induce creativity in your office? Write down three things that you can implement.

* http://sloanreview.mit.edu/article/how-innovative-is-your-companys-culture/

## DAY 3

> *I'm willing to try anything once. If I am passionate and consistent with my trials, I may stumble upon something wonderful!*

### Innovative Ideas

The following ideas from the *MIT Sloan Business Review* article that I mentioned yesterday might surprise you:

- **Behavior That Supports Innovation.** Cultures that support innovation are willing to shake things up, rather than cling to the status quo.
- **Challenging People to Take Risks.** Innovative climates encourage independent thinking and make it safe to take risks.
- **People Are the Most Important Resource.** Putting people above systems and projects have a powerful, positive impact on the culture.*

It can be a gamble to build your culture differently than others have done in the past, but it's likely worth it in the long run. Choose one of these ideas and implement it today. Then write down the results.

## DAY 4

> *When others doubt me, I will be a leader that defies the odds! I will help everyone around me to achieve feats that no one thought possible.*

### Go Crazy and Get Creative

One company that was studied in the *Sloane Management Review* article lived by these maxims:

* http://sloanreview.mit.edu/article/how-innovative-is-your-companys-culture/

- Encourage wild ideas.
- Defer judgment.
- Build on the ideas of others.
- Stay focused.

Cultures that foster creativity and innovation are fluid and curious, constantly asking questions and being willing to make changes based on the answers.

Choose one wild idea that shouldn't work and run with it. Make note as it progresses or fails, and learn from the experience.

## DAY 5

> *Even when the road seems bumpy, I will not stray from the company culture that I have built and that I am passionate about.*

### Shaping Your Company Culture

I remember my company's first warehouse. It was dirty, dusty, poorly lit (no windows for me to stare out of), and very poorly laid out. The only redeeming thing is we had a great landlord who gave us a break every once in a while when we couldn't make rent. The space was awful for workflow and productivity and ultimately for our company's culture.

We all know a vibrant company culture can result in better teamwork, motivation, and productivity. But the big questions are: Is it possible to shape and build your company culture? How do you do it? What can you do to ensure your team's high morale and happiness?

The short answer is yes, you can change a company's culture by doing a few things that might surprise you. In a recent short survey by a company called Turnstone, it was noted that out of 515 small business owners and managers, 90 percent of those surveyed believed that the physical environment and morale of a workplace heavily influence company culture.*

Write down what you feel your company culture is really about, and then ask some employees if they agree.

## DAY 6

> *I will inspire someone today.*

### An Inspiring Workplace Results in Inspired Work

In the same survey we talked about yesterday, 8 out of 10 people said that physical environment played a big role in company culture. The survey noted that conference rooms, kitchen space, and reception areas were just as important as the working space itself.

This makes sense, of course. Once you walk into any office, you immediately get a sense of a company's personality. Do they care about aesthetics? Are there cubicles or is the space open? All of these things affect how company culture is perceived.

In addition, employees all have different working styles and ways of being productive. One way to create a more inspiring space for workers is to give them options for their working space. Where do they want to sit? Would they rather sit or stand? What desk arrangement inspires them to be most productive? Making them feel more comfortable by tackling these questions can inspire your workers to create their best work.

Survey some more employees today. Ask them what would make work more inspiring for them. Learn the needs of those who are supporting you.

---

* http://myturnstone.com/blog/recent-turnstone-survey-confirms-office-culture-matters/

**DAY 7**

> *By cooperating with those around me, I will prove my loyalty to them. That loyalty will result in happy and efficient employees.*

## A Workplace with Good Morale Results in Happier Employees

The Turnstone survey also notes that workers are happier when physical and emotional well-being is promoted by their employers. Forty-seven percent of respondents said that giving employees small freedoms, such as the ability to display personal items on their desks, is an example of a gesture that will make employees feel more comfortable and welcomed. Business leaders are responsible for taking the lead and shaping their company cultures around positive morale.*

Once great culture is established, it is the business owner's responsibility to continually nurture it so that it stays vibrant. What do you think the tone of your company culture is?

---

* http://myturnstone.com/blog/recent-turnstone-survey-confirms-office-culture-matters/

# We Win!

It's easy to get excited about making a deal and to think about all of the things that you hope to get out of it. You are building a business, great things are on the horizon, and you are about to land a great deal. Sometimes we forget that someone else is even involved in the deal. This week you will find out how to approach deal-making discussions so they end in mutual satisfaction, leaving you and your company with a reputation that encourages even more clients to make deals with you.

## DAY 1

> *I will remember that winning is not always what it seems. Sometimes, losing is winning when it really comes down to it.*

### The Struggle Is Real

The next time you find yourself locked in a battle to get your way, here's a sure-fire strategy for you—forget about winning. Instead, figure out what would make your opposition feel like a winner.

First, try to think of the long-term mutual gain instead of gaining the short-term advantage. A win-win negotiation means a shared benefit for everyone involved, and it's the easiest way to close any deal. Forget about your own personal gain and concentrate on what will make both sides happy.

If you're currently involved in a tough negotiation, then write down what the other side has to gain by taking you up on your offer. Is it a fair deal for them? If not, then figure out what it would take to make it a true win-win.

**DAY 2**

> *The needs of others are more important*
> *than my own when it will solve a problem.*
> *Sometimes it is all about being humble.*

### A Win-Win Scenario

Now let's walk through a typical win-win scenario and how it plays out.

Start by setting a trusting, cooperative tone for the meeting right from the beginning. Negotiations are built on a foundation of trust and shared respect, so make it apparent that you're a person to be trusted. The best way to achieve this is to:

**1.** State your desire to achieve mutual benefit.
**2.** State your desire for a long-term relationship.
**3.** Insert the phrase "win-win" into your vocabulary.
**4.** Show proof of your honesty and willingness to serve.

Now let's think about that deal you're trying to close once again. Have you stated your desires for both sides to prosper yet? If not, spend some time thinking about how you can communicate those goals.

**DAY 3**

> *The art of negotiation is a technique and skill that I*
> *will work on daily and use to my advantage often.*

## Discuss the Issues

Discuss the issues using first-person plural pronouns (*we, our, us*). These words highlight your desire for mutual benefit and suggest a dedication toward teamwork.

Focus on interests, not positions. Positions are what you want; interests are how you get them. When you move from the "what" to the "why," you move from a potentially negative discussion (about demands) to a positive discussion (about common needs).

Come up with at least two sentences that move the "what" to the "why." Try and use them as soon as possible.

## DAY 4

> *As long as I express my concerns, it doesn't matter if I win or lose. I will be a winner as long as my voice has been heard.*

## Negotiate the Issues

Increase the number of issues you negotiate. This allows you to increase the chance for win-win outcomes by increasing the amount of matters you can resolve. Make it so both of you gain something of value.

Also, avoid ultimatums. A take-it-or-leave-it attitude creates pressure and limits options. Don't paint yourself or the other person into a corner. That would make it a win-lose scenario.

Write down a solution that you could use instead of giving an ultimatum. Then memorize it so it can be used to help back you (or the person you're negotiating with) out of a corner.

## DAY 5

> *Emotion is the worst thing I can bring to a negotiation. I will negotiate the facts and nothing more.*

## Give and Take

Give to get. Show your willingness to give and take as long as the other party is willing to do the same.

Don't get caught up in the emotion of the actual negotiation. Maintain your composure and objectivity. If you become angry, you lose.

Today, come up with some ways to stop being emotional during a heated conversation. This could be a breathing technique or memorizing a funny joke. Write your ideas down.

### DAY 6

> *I will be creative in learning how to get what I want and need, especially when I am negotiating. Finding the benefits for everyone involved is going to solve more problems than benefitting only myself.*

## It Takes Two

Engage in creative problem-solving. The problem you and the other party are trying to solve can be stated very simply: How can we arrive at a deal that maximizes our individual benefits, minimizes our individual losses, and is fair for both? Brainstorm all possible alternatives that achieve all three criteria. Then choose the alternative you both can live with.

You should also keep searching for ways to add value. Leave out no possibility to find ways to increase the value of what the other person wants—while keeping what you want.

How can you add value to the deal? How can you encourage problem-solving? Make some great notes about it! This is good stuff.

## DAY 7

> *It's easy to get your feelings hurt during a
> negotiation if you are not prepared. I will
> learn to leave my feelings at the door!*

### Compromise Creates Loyal Clients

Make concessions gradually and in increments. Small incremental moves are better than one sudden, large, and drastic move during the course of the negotiations. Smaller compromises are less threatening and easier to obtain.

Document all agreements. Avoid any possibility of a misunderstanding that would blow the whole deal. That would create a lose-lose scenario, and you will have wasted each other's time.

Write down all of the ideas that you will want to implement into your agreement. Be specific.

# Finding Focus

We all do it, every single day—multitasking. You have 10 things going at once and you feel like you are a productive ox. And for a moment, you may be, but multitasking is leading to burnout and you don't want to be the next casualty. This week, let's learn to help your team be more productive.

## DAY 1

> *The success of my organization is*
> *dependent on the success of my focus.*

### To Juggle or Not to Juggle

As an entrepreneur, I juggle things all day. When my partner and I started, we had no job descriptions and everyone did anything and everything. "Do more with less" has always been the way we had to operate to survive.

The result of this hyperconnectivity—multitasking and pushing our teams to the edge—is burnout. I see burnout in every business I visit as performance is emphasized, often at the expense of work/life balance, family, even physical health. Add multitasking to the picture and things can get even worse.

Let's just focus on the multitasking part for now . . . otherwise this could turn into a dissertation.

For years, multitasking has been touted as an indispensable facet of an employee's efforts. The theory revolved around the observation that busy workers who were able to apply themselves to several different projects at once had an advantage over others who couldn't or wouldn't do it. Motivational speakers still tout programs teaching multitasking to people to help them improve their ability and promising that it can transform their work and their futures.

Many studies have been conducted over the past two decades on this very subject. Researchers, business schools, and universities alike have all reached the same conclusion—any benefits that you think result directly from multitasking do not exist. It's a myth that multitasking is beneficial.

Write down some ways that you may be multitasking and not realizing it. Think hard!

## DAY 2

> *My mind is strong enough to be alert in any situation.*
> *I am confident in the strength of my mind.*

### This Is Your Brain on Multitasking

According to an in-depth report by Jon Hamilton from the National Public Radio newsletter (October 2008), we delude ourselves when we believe we can fully concentrate on several tasks at once.*

The research proves that our brains are capable of incredibly rapid changes of focus, but cannot fully focus on two or more different tasks simultaneously. Each task receives some attention, but the more tasks that are added to the mix, the more diluted the focus becomes. Whether anyone notices or not, this diluted concentration results in some tasks having less than desired outcomes. The issue worsens when the tasks are similar in nature; the brain uses the same area to deal with each.

Researchers have discovered that the brain acts as a manager when challenged with simultaneous tasks. It subconsciously decides which task deserves priority. In the days of the caveman, this would manifest

---

* http://www.npr.org/templates/story/story.php?storyId=95256794

as the fellow focusing on the approaching tiger and ignoring the bird he'd been hunting. Avoiding being the tiger's dinner was more important to survival.

In a modern office setting, an employee who tries to write an e-mail while talking with a client on the telephone will find his or her brain giving priority to the live person on the line. The employee simply can't do both tasks well simultaneously. The personal client interaction is more important to the worker's professional survival.

Do you remember a time that you screwed up in a conversation because you were multitasking? What could you have done differently?

## DAY 3

> *When there is pride involved, I will strive to assure that everyone involved feels successful. I can change the morale of any situation with my words.*

### Helping Multitasking Employees

What can a manager do to help workers who consistently try to multitask? It's an uphill battle since multitasking has become an area of pride for a lot of people.

You might consider these three suggestions:

1. Help employees to prioritize assignments. If everything is marked "urgent," then nothing actually is.
2. Encourage them to concentrate fully on the task in front of them. The more difficult the task, the more important the concentration.
3. When it's time to switch tasks, urge them to put the previous work away to avoid distraction and diluted concentration.

Focus and concentration are imperative for a superior performance. And a single job well done, rather than several poorly done, is a great antidote to potential burnout.

Prioritize something that you normally multitask. Write down what you will do and how you will do it.

## DAY 4

> *My employees are the bloodline of my business. As a leader, I will encourage them as often as I possibly can.*

### Lead Effectively

Truly successful leaders have learned that their business depends on their workers. The attitude of a leader affects every member of the team. A leader committed to adding value understands workers' stress and is personally invested in their growth and development. Delivering value as a leader does not involve criticizing, blaming, and belittling. It is focused on uplifting and enriching your workers to dream bigger and accomplish their goals.

How do you think that your attitude resonates? Write down some ways that you can keep a positive attitude in front of your employees so that they can continue to grow.

## DAY 5

> *In order to create dedicated employees, I will continue to place their feelings over my own as often as possible. I will recognize their successes daily.*

### Value What's Valuable

As mobile communication has grown, so has the workday of the average employee. E-mails, phone calls, and text messages now arrive at all hours of the day and night. Your business's success depends on the hard work and dedication of your employees. A leader must recognize the team's commitment and achievements.

Employees who feel recognized for their work and valued as individuals report greater job satisfaction, are more productive, and are more loyal to their employer.

Write down five ways to recognize your employees outside of the recognition programs that you've already implemented. It may seem like a lot, but it will help your productivity, I promise. It's redundant, but it works!

## DAY 6

> *As those that I associate with earn my respect,*
> *I will clearly communicate that fact with them.*
> *I will make sure that they know how much it*
> *means to me that we respect one another.*

### Add Value

Adding value means understanding that respect is the basis of all relationships. Greater respect is earned over time, but all members of the team deserve respect. After all, they would not be members of the team if they had not already shown promise.

As CEO of SAS John Goodnight stated, "Treat employees like they make a difference and they will." Respecting the talents and contributions of your team is vital to forging a mutually beneficial relationship.*

What talents shine brightest in your workplace? How can you accentuate those talents so your employees know that you recognize them?

## DAY 7

> *I will continually set new goals for*
> *myself and for my employees.*

### Consistent Reinforcement

Achieving your goals is not a onetime deal. As goals are reached, new goals should be set. Businesses and employees alike should constantly strive for greatness. Moving forward and dreaming bigger is achieved

---

* http://www.sas.com/en_us/company-information/great-workplace.html

only through reinforcement. Constantly reinforcing your values will allow you, your employees, and your business to achieve your desired results.

Leaders who add value build and sustain better relationships with their teams. They are genuine and sincere in helping their employees achieve their goals. Adding value means recognizing and respecting your employees, their dreams, their talents, and their contributions. Reinforcing those values leads to mutual success and loyal employees.

What employee goals do you recognize in your office? How can you make sure that you are reinforcing the values that you've laid out for your employees? Write about that tonight.

# Leveraging Loyalty

While loyalty programs are not going to disappear, the future of customer loyalty can be seen in two trends that will reshape the way they function. This week we will study these two trends and discover ways you can use them in your business to drive customer engagement.

## DAY 1

> *Loyalty is something that I will give and will also receive. Creating loyalty among my customers is something that I will strive for every day.*

### The Loyalty Model

It seems that nowadays everyone is collecting customer loyalty points at their favorite store. How many little plastic cards are on your key chain? Grocery stores, pharmacies, gas stations, restaurants, hotels, airlines—all have reward systems designed to keep you coming back. Points, discounts, and free products encourage your loyalty.

The loyalty model has been a successful business tool ever since American Airlines introduced the first mileage plan in 1981. How successful? According to Colloquy Research, the average US household now takes part in 21.9 loyalty programs every year.*

---

* http://adage.com/article/digitalnext/mobile-shaking-traditional-loyalty-marketing-programs/296086/

Think about a loyalty program that you have for your customers. Do you even have one? Write down some ideas.

## DAY 2

> *I will provide a service or product that*
> *people want to represent and are proud of.*
> *Their loyalty will define my success.*

### The Future of Customer Loyalty

While loyalty programs are not going to disappear, the future of customer loyalty can be seen in trends that will reshape the way they function. No more little plastic cards. Instead, smart businesses will add more personalized offers based on data about individual preferences, like discounts delivered automatically to mobile phones.

Starbucks has had a successful loyalty program since 2008 when customers could register a gift card and receive free soy milk, Internet access, and refills on drip coffee. With the mobile app, launched in early 2011, customers now get discounts when they pay with their app and automatic calculations of points. By 2016, 21 percent of transactions made in the United States were paid using the mobile app.*

How can you jump on this trend? Write some ideas down and research them.

## DAY 3

> *When my customers are happy, my*
> *employees are happy, and I am happy.*

---

* http://www.fool.com/investing/general/2016/01/26/just-how-big-is-starbucks-mobile-order-pay-and-wha.aspx

## Personalize It!

Walmart and Walgreens use apps to make personalized offers to shoppers as they're in the store. American Express also recently announced a partnership with Uber, the taxi service company. Under the program, when customers pay with AmEx when using Uber, they earn twice the AmEx rewards points—and can use those points to pay for future Uber rides.

Do you have a way for your customers to earn "points" for your product or services? Do any of these ideas coincide with the ideas you wrote down yesterday? Try to combine ideas today.

## DAY 4

> *I will strive to secure customers that know how*
> *important they are to my company. Whatever it takes,*
> *I will reward that loyalty as long as possible.*

## Make Your Clients Feel Important

Everyone likes to feel important. Nordstrom has known this for decades; each customer is treated with respect and unsurpassed service. The challenge of building loyalty by providing an exceptional experience is that every customer is different. This can mean different styles, different budgets, and different needs. Figure out how to listen to the customer and an authentic, lifetime loyalty is established.

How can you make each customer feel important? Try to think of something that makes each customer feel like you've created the program specifically for him or her.

## DAY 5

> *I am the leader of a company and I will behave
> in a way that is optimistic, happy, and fun.
> Today, I am going to be sure that I portray each
> of those qualities throughout my day.*

### Be Inspired

Apple stores are known for their inviting way of letting customers "play" with the products. Associates, who are not paid with commissions, are available to explain the products and teach on the spot. Customers can request as much assistance as they need or none at all. It's a positive experience every time.

What inspiration can you draw from Apple's approach toward its customers? How can you be innovative in increasing your customer loyalty through this kind of approach?

## DAY 6

> *I will create magic today.*

### Be Magical

Disney parks are the ultimate family vacation because guests are always treated to a warm, friendly environment. Each interaction, from character to groundskeeper, is perfect. People return well into adulthood to recapture that "magical" feeling.

Do you have something "magical" that you can offer your customers? How can you turn your product or service into a feeling that people will relate to it? Explore some ideas today.

## DAY 7

> *I am authentic and pure. Because of this, people trust me and my brand. I will continue to be each of those things in hopes that I can inspire more people to do the same.*

### The Future of Loyalty

Harley-Davidson has created a loyalty program for motorcycle fans that is unmatched. Customers can build their own Harleys, participate in events, and wear "Bad never looked so good" clothing. By establishing a prestigious lifestyle loyalty program, customers will never go anywhere else.

So, what about those little plastic cards on your key chain? While they have been useful, look for improved versions to build stronger customer loyalty in the future. What do you want to try next?

# The Sales Superstar

Selling takes discipline, a system, and an ability to communicate and understand people. Do you and the people who work for you have what it takes to be superstars in sales?

## DAY 1

> *I am confident in my ability to sell myself and my company. I have what it takes to be the best!*

### Build Rapport

One of the biggest fears many people have is selling something to other people; many people say they don't want to come across as pushy. But as a business owner and manager, you have to sell to survive. Good salespeople sell without coming across as pushy. The most effective selling strategy has three stages: building a foundation, setting expectations, and following up.

People buy from someone they like. Some people are able to establish rapport faster than others. Take the time to build some common ground with the person you are hoping to sell to. The shorter the sales cycle the more difficult this is, but it is still possible even in an environment in which the sales cycle is extremely short. The more common ground you can find in a short amount of time the better rapport you'll develop. This is the cornerstone of building a foundation and establishing rapport. With this solidly in place, you can genuinely feel like you are helping your potential client and not pushing something on him or her. In turn, those clients can sense that you genuinely care and want to help them with a need that they have.

Think of one client specifically and write down how you can build a better rapport with that client.

## DAY 2

> *When the big picture is blurry, I will refocus*
> *and rebuild until it is clear again.*

### Build Reciprocity

Keeping a view of the big picture will help you stay focused and positive. The reality is that the person you are building rapport with may not turn out to be your ideal client but may know someone who is. Referrals are the best prospects, and a great way to get referrals is to generate as many relationships as possible that have some form of reciprocity.

A wise person once said, "The nicest thing you can do for someone is be nice to the people they love." If you can find creative ways to do nice things for a person's children, nieces, nephews, significant other, and friends, then you will be building an enormous bank of reciprocity. Not only that, but it also feels really good and you're making the world a better place.

How can you make the world a better place? Think of one area where you can implement a referral. Write it down and write the referral today!

## DAY 3

> *Where there is a need, I will see an opportunity!*

## Uncover the Need and Gauge Interest

There are probably many people out there who need your product or service. Some of them may know it and some of them may not. The reality is that other business owners are probably going after the same clients that you are. A good approach is to use a two-prong strategy (attempt to sell to both types of people). It is obviously a little harder to sell to the latter category, but you will have less competition.

When targeting potential clients who don't realize they need your product, you first have to help them see the bigger picture and how you can help. Once you uncover the need with probing, thought-provoking questions, then (and only then) you can focus on how you can meet that need better than anyone else.

You can only help people who want to be helped. Visualize a lifeguard swimming out to help someone who is drowning. If the person doesn't want your help or is not fighting to save himself or herself, then you won't be able to help. Even worse, the person may drag you down to the bottom of the lake.

The degree of receptivity someone has to your product or service will determine the expectations you both will have going forward. The ability to successfully gauge interest is the first step to setting expectations.

How can you be more receptive? Write down at least three ways.

## DAY 4

> *No matter how successful I am, I will*
> *always keep my expectations high.*

## Set Expectations of Frequency

Whether people say it or not, they have expectations about everything in life. Figuring out what those expectations *really* are can be challenging.

Here is the secret to success. ASK! That is the only way to find out. If the answer is ambiguous, then ask a couple of questions to clarify what the person means. Then set something in stone. For example, "I'll call you Tuesday the 25th at noon." If this feels shaky and awkward, then the foundation you built up to this point may not be strong enough. Sometimes the only way to tell if something is strong enough to support what you put on top of it is by testing it.

Everyone also has a preferred method of communication. A great question to ask someone is how he or she would like for you to contact them (call, text, e-mail, etc.). People will appreciate your thoughtfulness and you will set the expectation at the same time. If the person tells you the preference is e-mails, then you can follow up immediately with, "How often would you like for me to follow up with you in case you are extremely busy and can't get back to me at that moment?"

Today, write down a thoughtful e-mail response that can be edited and tailored to various customers and prospects.

## DAY 5

*Even when the idea is small, I will write it down. I will document my thoughts daily.*

### Keep It in Writing

As much as possible, keep your follow-up in writing; whether this means texts, e-mails, or letters. This creates a paper trail that often comes in handy. There's an old cynical joke that goes something like: What's the difference between love and e-mail? E-mail lasts forever.

With a paper trail (e-mail, text, or mobile messaging apps) you can confirm that your follow-up has been sent, delivered, and in many cases read. This will come in handy many times when the client says you never followed up.

Check out some new mobile messaging apps that track your messages. Do you think you can implement one of these? Why or why not?

## DAY 6

> *I will not leave any room for discrepancy when*
> *it comes to my clients and customers, even if I*
> *have bad news. I will always be direct.*

### Keep It Direct

By keeping your follow-up direct with the client, you don't have to worry about your message getting lost in translation or in the shuffle of life.

There are circumstances in which a client may say he or she prefers you follow up with someone else (an assistant, a spouse, etc.); this can be a good thing or a bad thing. Some people recognize that their assistants are more trustworthy with follow-up items than they are—in this situation working with the assistants is probably better. However, there are times when being passed off to the assistant is one way of blowing people off.

Write down one statement that you use often that is indirect. How can you make it more direct? Now write down a new way to make the statement.

## DAY 7

> *My world will be better if there are no enemies in it.*

### Keep Friends Close . . . Assistants Closer

There is a way to make being blown off a good thing. If you're able to turn an assistant into a friend, then you're in a great position.

If you see gatekeepers or assistants as enemies, then you've already lost. Attempt to turn them into friends and have them help you in the follow-up process with the person you are attempting to sell to. A great way to do this without coming across as too pushy is to figure out a creative way to do something nice for the people the gatekeeper cares about (e.g., a hat for their child or a gift card for ice cream on a hot summer day).

You're bound to make a mistake every once in a while during these three stages of polite persistence. When that happens, apologize to your client and try to refine what he or she wants in terms of communication. In this setting, it never hurts to ask. It shows three things: you realize something is wrong, you're listening, and you care. All three of these things are extremely effective with your customer.

Write about one time when you felt like you made a mistake while being persistent. What could you have done differently? Write that down too so that you don't forget!

# Helpful Hints

When a potential client invites you to an event, it's important to show up enthusiastic and ready to participate. Whether it's a Halloween party or a Thanksgiving feast, you need to be prepared when it comes to showing up versus blowing up at a party! That's right, even if you get an invitation to an "ugly sweater" party, dig out your worst sweater or head to the store.

## DAY 1

> *There is always an opportunity to network. I will find one, no matter what day it is!*

### Networking Know-How

You know a holiday is near when an invitation comes for one of those parties that you dread every year. But with all the parties and events during the various holidays, you should take advantage of the festive mood, whatever the season, to do some of your best networking.

Have you planned anything for an upcoming holiday? If not, write down some ideas. It can be the Fourth of July or New Year's Eve, but you should plan because social outings during any holiday are a wonderful way to connect, sell, and network. Throughout this week, we will learn some more ways to use the holidays to your advantage. You will receive far more than a lump of coal if you follow my advice!

## DAY 2

*I will plan for whatever holiday is approaching. I don't want to miss an opportunity because I did not plan ahead.*

### Plan Ahead

When you have an event to attend, decide on a goal for the evening. Two new contacts? Four introductions? With a plan in mind, you'll be motivated to move around and spend time with more people than your usual pals. Bring some business cards, but hand them out only when appropriate or when asked. It is, after all, a party.

Write down your goals for the next holiday that you come across. Don't stretch yourself but still try to push yourself to the limit. What can you gain this season other than a few pounds?

## DAY 3

*It may be a stretch for me, but I will try harder to go with the flow.*

### Go with the Theme

If you get an invitation to a costume party, then try to make your costume the most memorable of the group. If it's a cocktail party, then you dress the part there too. Some parties include a toy or book drive; don't neglect your chance to give to the less fortunate. It's important to show up enthusiastic and ready to participate. Make sure to wear a smile, too. No Scrooges allowed!

What can you do to shine at the next event that you are invited to? If it's a graduation party or a wedding shower, tailor your gift so that it leaves just a hint of your business along with it. Write down some ideas on how you can tailor gifts to support your business without being overbearing.

## DAY 4

> *Although each holiday provides a time to celebrate,*
> *more than anything, I will celebrate self-control.*

### Know Your Limits

The eggnog may be the best you've ever had, but you need a clear head if you're going to meet new people and make a good impression. A drink or two is fine, but you'll have a hard time regaining credibility if you "win" the shot contest and end up passed out on the floor.

Have you ever lost an opportunity because you didn't know your limits? Think about how it affected you and what you could have done to avoid the situation. Write it down.

## DAY 5

> *My personality will lead me to the right people, and I will*
> *trust myself when it comes to discussing things with them.*

### Wait to Talk About Your Business

People want to relax and enjoy the party. Lead off with an easy and non-controversial topic or question: "How do you know Bob and Mary?" "Wow! That is really an ugly sweater!" "Isn't the village light display lovely this year?" Once you've started a conversation, it can eventually lead to the topic of what you each do for a living.

Write down one conversation starter that is related to the next event or holiday that is on your calendar. Tailor it to include something that will lead to talk about your business.

## DAY 6

> *Great conversation will lead to great relationships*
> *and great deals. I will not miss out!*

## Position Yourself

Standing near the food is a surefire way to meet others. Everyone heads to the buffet at some point.

"Aren't these bacon-wrapped scallops delicious?" "I wonder where she got this potato salad." Even the shyest person is comfortable talking about food.

Another way to meet someone is to approach a person standing alone. Not only are you helping someone who may not know anyone else, you may discover a fascinating contact.

Research the person that invites you to the next party that you will go to. Look at that person's Facebook or LinkedIn page and be a "stalker" (as they call it these days). Does that person have any connections that you might want to meet because of business? Write down the person's name so that you don't forget.

## DAY 7

> *My manners are the first representation that I have to show others what my company is about.*

## Remember Your Etiquette

Bring a bottle of wine or small gift to the hosts. Never leave the party without finding them and thanking them. Send a handwritten note the next day. A polite guest always gets invited back . . . for more networking opportunities!

Of course, you're there to have fun. And you can also do some good networking with people you might not have otherwise met. Happy holidays!

One last tip: Don't wait for someone to plan a holiday party or event, plan one yourself and utilize it to the advantage of your business. Write down an idea now!

# Calm and Collective

It happens to everyone. No matter what our business, we may all encounter a crisis. It comes out of nowhere: an accident, a breakdown, a lawsuit. The immediate panic is overwhelming, followed quickly by feelings of despair and helplessness and a need to do something.

Earlier we talked about how to stay productive during a crisis, but now let's talk about how to deal with the crisis itself.

## DAY 1

> *Staying calm is not always easy, but I can learn to do so. When a crisis arises, I will develop a method of remaining calm.*

### Keep Calm

Before you respond, learn how to stay calm in a crisis. It can make all the difference in the outcome, no matter what the cause.

Stop, look, and listen. Resist the temptation to react or retaliate. Take a few seconds to evaluate. You need to determine the full scope of the situation before proceeding. (Of course a sudden or physical threat, such as a fire or a colleague's heart attack, requires immediate action.)

Who, what, when, where, and how. Think like a news reporter and get as much data as possible. Delegate responsibilities to get the job accomplished as quickly as possible. Depending on the crisis, a public announcement or response may be expected, so time is critical.

Write down a generic response to your customers and employees that you can use during a crisis.

## DAY 2

> *I will learn to deal with unplanned events*
> *as though I planned them. Calmly, instinctively,*
> *and in a way that reminds my employees*
> *that I am a great leader.*

### Accept Risks

Everything has a level of risk, from learning to ride a bicycle to trying a new hairstyle. When you own a small business, you know you're accepting risks. There will be some you're aware of and some that will be surprises. As a smart entrepreneur, you don't let this stop you from weighing the facts and making the best possible choices.

And if things don't go as planned? Well, you develop a new strategy from a wiser perspective.

Gather your team. You'll need people who can stay focused and positive. No naysayers or blamers. Now you're able to analyze the problem, and begin to get answers and solutions. How you handle the crisis will impact your company brand. There have been companies that have actually benefited from immediate and adept action.

Who will be on your crisis team? Make a list.

## DAY 3

> *When I am nervous or afraid, I will communicate those*
> *feelings to my employees. I will be honest at all times.*

### Communicate Honestly

Don't stall on keeping stakeholders informed; your company reputation depends on clear and timely responsiveness. A lack of communication only increases anxiety and damages the business. Honesty is essential. Never, ever lie or mislead.

If you've hired well, or have close advisors, you can trust their doubts. Are they seeing something concerning in a contract, employee, vendor, or opportunity? It's easy to dismiss others' opinions, but you need to listen. They have your best interest at heart, even if you don't want to hear it.

Write down a list of the first people that you want or need to inform when something major happens.

## DAY 4

*If I need a breather, I will take a breather.*

### Take Care of Yourself

Looking out for yourself and others who are directly involved is critical during a crisis. Even a short break or time away allows people to clear their heads and see their families. Eat well and avoid excess caffeine or alcohol. Try to get adequate rest.

The truth is, you can't grow and succeed without legal advice. Hire an accountant. Before a crisis strikes, form a limited liability company (LLC) to limit any liabilities, rather than have your personal finances be at stake. Have an attorney review your contracts. Yes, it costs money, but you can't afford not to protect yourself. Chances are that at some point, you will be glad you had the foresight to hire professionals.

Write down the names of the lawyer and accountant that you think would work best in a crisis situation. If you don't know one, do some research and find one!

## DAY 5

> *In every case and every crisis there is something to learn.*
> *I will learn from even the most difficult situations.*

### Look to Others for a Sounding Board

Seek advice from mentors and trusted colleagues. People who know you well can serve as sounding boards. They may also have a fresh perspective that you hadn't considered. Sometimes, they will have had similar experiences and can help you strategize.

"Mentoring programs play a key role in decreasing employee turnover," said a 2013 study published in the *Journal of Vocational Behavior*.* It discovered that people who have the opportunity to serve as mentors experience greater job satisfaction and a higher commitment to their employers. On the other side, people being mentored experienced a lot less stress since they had a trusted advisor to turn to.

Who will be your mentor during a crisis? Does that person know? Write that name down and have a conversation with that person so that you can get some tips on what to do if the "what-if" ever happens.

## DAY 6

> *I am the example that others will follow. I*
> *will represent my company culture at all times*
> *by remaining calm, strong, and honest.*

### Conduct a Postcrisis Debriefing

After the situation has been resolved, do an extensive study. Ask a quality expert to help you with a "root cause analysis" to fully dissect what happened and what can be done to prevent a reoccurrence. Find out how you can benefit from the crisis.

---

* http://www.sciencedirect.com/science/journal/00018791/85

Risk is necessary. In fact, it can be exhilarating and take you to the next level. But it always needs to be carefully considered. Remember: Mark Zuckerberg wouldn't have succeeded without risk. Here's hoping you use risk to become the next phenomenal business!

Write down your debriefing plan today.

## DAY 7

> *Nothing can stop a great leader. Even a crisis presents an opportunity to grow.*

### Don't Panic!

When an unexpected event threatens your business, don't panic. Step forward and face it, since this is the only way to learn some lessons that can strengthen your team and your company.

Use what you've learned this week and develop a full crisis plan. It can cover who takes charge of public communications, how to direct calls or questions to key staff, how to report a potential crisis, and how to conduct an investigation. A proactive policy can reduce chaos and confusion.

# *Break, Brake, Breathe*

Sometimes you might feel as though taking a breather is impossible. Your plate is full and heavy, and you simply cannot stop carrying it everywhere you go. You are headed down a dark path that ends with burnout. If you burn out, you can expect to lose even more working hours than you would have if you had just taken a break. This week, let's learn about taking time for the little things and how that will help your heavy workload in the long run.

## DAY 1

> *I am just as important to my family*
> *as I am to my business.*

### Resolved and Resolute

I have resolved to spend more time with those I love and to spend more time pursuing some of my hobbies that I've had no time to really enjoy since I started my business eight years ago. The other resolution I have integrated into my life is to do more moving and less sitting in front of a screen.

Write down a couple of things that you are going to try and resolve to do this year. They can involve your business or simply yourself. Make sure that you dig deep and write down things that you can accomplish and that are attached to you significantly. If you resolve to do something that you are not passionate about, it is likely that you will not succeed with your resolution. Find your passion and write about exactly what it is that you want to happen in the next several months.

## DAY 2

> *I will learn to balance my priorities, both in my personal life and my business life.*

### Take a Break

When you own a business (or just really love what you do), you probably find yourself working all of the time. However, it is important to have hobbies and passions outside of work. It is healthy to get out of the office and spend time doing other things. Believe me once I started taking a break and making time for other things my work got better.

Make a list of some things that you can start to do outside of your business, whether they are hobbies, family activities, or physical activities that will help your health. Now choose one. Only one. Focus on this first activity and strive to do it for the remainder of this week at a minimum.

## DAY 3

> *It's vital for me to find time for those I love. The people I love are my number one priority.*

### Don't Miss Out!

When you continue to work late, you miss out on your family and friends. They will gradually get the hint that you are not interested in them and stop asking you to spend time with them. Eventually when you are interested in spending time with them, they will no longer be available to spend time with you.

Make a list of the things that you are missing when you spend too much time at work. Will you have the opportunity to participate in those things again, or are they significant events that you cannot get back? Was it worth missing? Did you get so much done that it was worth the loss?

## DAY 4

> *I cannot nourish my mind without a nourished body. Today I will focus on the fuel that I provide to my body and pay attention to the things I eat.*

### You Are What You Eat

What do you eat when you work late? For a lot of people, the answer is takeout and fast food. You should be eating at home more so that your diet is healthier. Take a good look at your overall health. Is it affected by what you eat? Is what you eat directly related to how much time that you spend at work?

Do a little research today and find some statistics on health. Research the life spans of entrepreneurs who know how to take a break and those who live in the office. Who lives longer? How long do you want to live? Are your hours in the office worth years of your life?

## DAY 5

> *I need to move! Today I will move at least five minutes longer than I did yesterday.*

### MOVE!

People who work late are less likely to exercise. Exercise is an important part of life, especially for people who have sedentary jobs. You need to get up and moving instead of sitting all day in front of your computer. So, make sure that you find time to fit some exercise in every day, even if you just take a walk during your lunch break. All movement counts.

259

Write down what exercises you are currently doing and which ones you'd like to implement.

Once again, think about your longevity. How will you get to the office if you can't climb a flight of stairs or walk from your car because you are so out of shape? Write down exactly what you are going to do to make a change. Then stick to it!

## DAY 6

> *I must learn to love things other than my business. My focus today will revolve around learning to be passionate in another arena.*

### Do What You Love

Hobbies and passions will help you find good stress relief. After a few hours (or even a day) away, you might come back to your work much more refreshed and ready to accomplish a difficult task. Sometimes, when you get stuck, all you need is a break and you might find the answer right in front of you.

Remember that activity you were supposed to try? Have you been trying it? How does it make you feel? Are you more successful in the workplace now that you are taking a break?

## DAY 7

> *In order to continue to love my job, I have to separate it from my personal life. I want to continue to love both so I will find a balance.*

### Avoid Burnout

Burnout is common when people do not take breaks from their work. Instead, you work and work until you get tired of doing what you used to love. Work starts becoming boring and something that you do not want to do anymore.

Working 20 hours a day is unhealthy. It causes you to eat unhealthy food and sit too much. You lose out on time with your family and friends. You don't exercise, and you can lose the passion for your business. So take a break; go walk the dog or throw the ball with your kid. You'll be more focused and ready to get back to work. Implement some kind of break in your day today. Whatever it is, make sure it is outside of your comfort zone and something that you would not normally do. Don't avoid it, and make sure that you try and enjoy it. Add it to your schedule in the following weeks!

# The Accomplished Attitude

There are ways to avoid burnout, but you need to know the common pitfalls that can threaten your personal well-being. These things are a major influencer on your everyday effectiveness.

Contributors to burnout are sloppy time management, poor boundaries, stress, emotional burnout, and boredom syndrome. This week we will explore each of these pitfalls and learn ways to prevent burnout and thrive every day in your work.

## DAY 1

> *If I can't manage my time, I can't manage my business. I am capable of managing my time wisely.*

### Fix Sloppy Time Management

Not paying enough attention to time management can contribute significantly to burnout and imbalance. People who don't pace themselves to accommodate breaks in their work schedules don't allow sufficient time just for themselves and are inviting burnout. A sloppy approach to time management prevents you from giving your best, and it creates a more stressful environment for yourself. In other words, it makes sense to work smarter, not harder.

Be sure to set aside 20 minutes every day for planning and thinking—whether it is about your business agreements, goals, marketing, client relations, or evaluating what is working and what is not.

Think before you leap. Life is much more enjoyable and successful when one is coming from a proactive position than one of reaction. Write about what you learned during your 20 minutes.

## DAY 2

> *Boundaries are necessary to run a successful company. I will adhere to any boundaries that I have set for myself; no excuses!*

### Set Clear Boundaries

We talked about setting boundaries before, but now let's revisit them and see if you are keeping up.

The inability to effectively maintain and manage boundaries with clients, coworkers, and management is the leading cause of burnout. Boundaries help to protect the respect and dignity of each person. Resentment builds if you frequently allow your boundaries to be crossed.

For instance, you may encounter situations where others are prone to take advantage of your good nature and generosity. Learn to set strong boundaries for yourself. Practice saying no. Create policies and adhere to them. Make a note about how you can work with a supervisor in your company or meet regularly with colleagues for peer supervision and evaluation.

## DAY 3

> *A strong mind stems from a strong body. One cannot function without the other. I will maintain both!*

### Take Time for Self-Care

Do stretches, take breaks, do breathing exercises, make adjustments in your body mechanics, eat properly, meditate, or do martial arts. Walk your talk. If you are a dentist, make sure your teeth are in great shape.

If you are a nutritional consultant, eat healthy foods. How can you realistically expect clients to be convinced to regularly incorporate your services into their lives if you aren't practicing what you preach?

Let's talk about that meditation you were going to do in a prior week. Did it work? If not, maybe you need to try something different. Riding a bike and implementing a yoga program are two great ways to relax. Do some research on some relaxing activities and choose one.

Keep balance in mind as the key to stress management. You need to keep things in perspective. Don't react to things that aren't your responsibility. Learn to deal with interruptions, and learn how to say no.

## DAY 4

> *If I push myself too far, I may say or do*
> *something I will regret. I will balance my world*
> *so that I don't reach that breaking point.*

### Avoid Emotional Burnout

Emotional burnout is a bit trickier. Attitude plays a critical role. You can avoid burnout by making time to meet with colleagues on a regular basis, attending conferences, varying the way you work, maintaining a strong personal support system, and enrolling in new classes to expand your knowledge and stay inspired. Set boundaries by learning to express your needs clearly and honestly so others know you expect to be treated with respect and dignity.

Do you feel like you are emotionally burnt out? What can you do to inspire yourself? Write down three things that inspire you and make sure that you think about them the next time you start a project.

## DAY 5

> *It's time to switch up my routine! Today*
> *I will do something different.*

### Steer Clear of Ruts

People who have been in business for many years may find themselves falling prey to boredom syndrome. Sometimes a great routine turns into a deep rut. Here are some suggestions to avoid this kind of burnout:

- Alter your work environment.
- Start a whole new business.
- Learn new skills.
- Take a sabbatical.
- Volunteer your services.
- Revamp your business plan.

Keep in mind every career has its ups and downs. The key is to recognize the difference between a natural phase and a downward spiral. Step back and objectively evaluate the situation. Determine why you are encountering boredom and what might work to remedy it. After you have assessed the situation and brainstormed possible solutions, discuss the issue with an advisor. Getting feedback from a trusted advisor can often shed new light on a challenging situation.

A few changes to your routine and mindset can make a world of difference. Choose one thing from the list above and write about how that change will help you in the long run.

## DAY 6

> *Today I will focus on only good, happy*
> *thoughts. No other thoughts are allowed.*

## Stay Positive

Theresa Glomb, a work and organizations professor at the University of Minnesota's Carlson School of Management, explains, "Good things are about three to five times more frequent than bad things at work, but bad events have about five to 10 times the impact as good things."*

Here's how to end every day on a positive note: Find something in your day to be grateful for.

Did you get a new client? Enjoy lunch with coworkers? Receive a compliment on your presentation? Don't let an unpleasant incident determine your mood after you leave the office. Jot down a few things in your daily planner that made you happy or that went well. Write just one positive thing on a slip of paper and put it in a jar; then review those slips at the end of the month or year. Or, put a dollar in that jar as you recall what you're grateful for that day—and buy yourself a treat when you reach $100!

Also, learn to take a break from social media. It's fun to catch up with friends on Facebook, Instagram, Twitter, or Pinterest. It can also be stressful, and actually lead to discontent if you start comparing your life to others' or spend too much time browsing on the Internet versus engaging in face-to-face interactions. Do a quick check, but don't spend your entire evening online.

Write your first positive thought down right now. If you have two, then write two. Try to keep doing it to remind yourself of all of the positive aspects of what you are doing.

## DAY 7

*Today, it's all about me. I have worked hard to get to where I am and I am going to celebrate that!*

---

* https://www.entrepreneur.com/article/240316

## End Your Day with Exercise and a Good Book

Contrary to the belief that evening exercise can interfere with sleep, a 2013 study shows that exercise anytime has benefits.* Something as small as a walk before or after dinner can lift your mood and relieve tension. If you're able to get outside in the fresh air; all the better.

A good way to end each day is to find something that will remind you how fortunate you are, as well as inspire you to continue to do great work. What you choose is entirely personal. It could be a book of daily affirmations, a biography of your personal hero, a religious or spiritual book, or Shakespeare's sonnets. Whatever your meaningful choice, give yourself the gift of a few minutes to read and reflect before turning out the light.

No matter how hard you work, there are never enough hours in the day. Some tasks will be carried over until tomorrow. Instead, strive for balance between your work and your personal life. Remember how important each is to you. You need both!

Research inspirational books, long or short, and choose one to begin reading. Write down why you chose it and commit to reading one chapter a day.

* http://articles.mercola.com/sites/articles/archive/2014/05/08/late-night-exercise.aspx

# *Instant Impressions*

Imagine that you're preparing for an important meeting. Everything seems perfect. Your hair looks great, your new suit fits well, and your shoes are polished. You've done everything possible to make a good first impression. But some things are beyond our control. Everyone we meet will make assumptions about us . . . and we will do the same about them. This week focuses on ways to make a great first impression.

## DAY 1

> *I will seize every opportunity that*
> *I have to make a great impression.*

### Be Ready!
- Thirty-three percent of managers know within 90 seconds if they will hire you.*
- People will determine if you're trustworthy within one-tenth of a second.†
- Before the brain registers your gender, it has already decided if you are likable.‡

---

\* http://theundercoverrecruiter.com/infographic-how-interviewers-know-when-hire-you-90-seconds/
† https://www.entrepreneur.com/article/242880
‡ http://www.hireology.com/blog/interview-scorecards-3-ways-to-avoid-bias

"There can be as much value in the blink of an eye as in months of rational analysis." wrote Malcolm Gladwell, in his bestseller *Blink: The Power of Thinking without Thinking*. Gladwell introduced the concept of "thin slicing," the lightening-quick process of deciding characteristics, from attractiveness to intelligence to financial success.

Knowing about thin slicing can help you influence what people decide about you within seconds of meeting you, and how to make a great first impression.

Write down a list of things that make a bad first impression when you meet someone. Have you ever done any of those things?

## DAY 2

> *Today I will focus on listening to what other people think of me, good or bad, and I will learn from it.*

### Respect Yourself

Pay attention to how you dress for any type of encounter. Remember nonverbal cues account for 55 percent of all communication.* Wearing ill-fitting, wrinkled, or inappropriate clothing sends the message that you don't care how you look . . . and that you probably have a messy work ethic as well. Don't neglect grooming either. Clean nails and neat hair indicate pride in appearance.

You are representing your business and your company. You are the brand. Write down three things you can do differently when it comes to your appearance.

## DAY 3

> *Today I will change the status quo!*

* http://www.nonverbalgroup.com/2011/08/how-much-of-communication-is-really-nonverbal

### Be Proud of Your Status

Power and status are perceived by how you dress and how you move. *Business Insider* reported the results of a Canadian study that revealed how well-dressed people earn more money and are promoted more often.* Stand up straight, with your shoulders back, to indicate confidence and success. Develop a firm handshake to establish instant rapport.

When you meet people for the first time, what do you tell them your title is? I know you are an entrepreneur, but are you the president of the company? CEO? What's your actual title? Write down some different ideas of titles that brag about your status.

## DAY 4

> *I am adaptable. I am confident in my intelligence,*
> *and I am ready to change the world!*

### Be Intelligent

A study done by Nora A. Murphy, PhD, at Loyola Marymount University found that eye contact is a key factor in how your intelligence is perceived. "Looking while speaking was a key behavior," she wrote. "It significantly correlated with IQ, was successfully manipulated by impression-managing targets, and contributed to higher perceived intelligence ratings."† Another tip: Raise your eyebrows! By opening your eyes slightly more than normal, you'll create the "eyebrow flash" that is the universal signal of recognition and acceptance.

Spend a few minutes practicing speaking in front of a mirror. At first don't do anything different, but eventually begin to do the eyebrow flash. Talk to yourself as though you were speaking to a customer. Write down the things that you need to change in order to make others perceive that you've got great intelligence and you aren't afraid to show it!

---

* http://www.businessinsider.com/how-to-instantly-appear-successful-2015-2
† https://www.advisory.com/daily-briefing/2015/01/16/trying-to-look-smart-often-backfires-heres-how-to-do-it-right

## DAY 5

> *It is possible to maintain a good attitude even*
> *in a bad situation. I will be genuine today.*

### Be Liked

Your attitude is everything; people will read it immediately. A genuine smile says, "I'm friendly and nonthreatening." Offer a smile with your handshake, and use eye contact to show interest and openness. (Notice each person's eye color to improve your eye contact.) When sitting, lean in slightly to indicate curiosity and engagement.

While you are the entrepreneur, it's also important for you to sell yourself. Even if you are nervous, coming across with a positive attitude and a genuine personality will make the person you are speaking with empathetic of you.

So find a friend and practice engaging with him or her. Then write down three ways that you can focus on engagement during conversation.

## DAY 6

> *I will celebrate my successes and learn from my failures.*

### Eliminate Failure Before It Happens

Sometimes you have to tell yourself what is *not* going to happen in order to accomplish what you want to happen.

When you meet a person, tell yourself what is not going to happen. You will not spit, you will not laugh inappropriately, and you will not belch. Prepare yourself for all of the things that you will not do, and you will be more likely to avoid them and maintain the presence that you are hoping for. You only get one first impression.

By eliminating the opportunity for failure, you include the possibility of success. Write down your list of the things you will *not* do when making a first impression.

## DAY 7

> *I am so thankful for every moment that I am blessed with and I will live my life exuding thanks to others.*

### Be Grateful

Having gratitude has shown to have positive impacts on all the pleasure centers of our brain. The reward network rooted deep inside of our mind is hard-wired for gratitude. In her study entitled "Why People Take Risks to Help Others: Altruism's Roots in the Brain," Abigail Marsh, associate professor at Georgetown University, wrote:

> The amygdala in altruists is supersensitive to fear or distress in another's face . . . They showed this very specific increase in amygdala activation in response to others' fear. Conversely, the amygdala in a psychopath's brain is significantly smaller. The brain's emotional radar in psychopaths was blunted and relatively unresponsive to someone else's distress or fear.*

Make sure the person that you are meeting with can tell how thankful you are that he or she spent time with you. Write down three ways that you can show gratitude when you are making a first impression. Remember, you may only have seconds to make that first impression, so make sure it's not some long-winded thank-you.

* http://www.npr.org/templates/transcript/transcript.php?storyId=349639464

# Changing Your Own Reflection

Our final week together is going to be about reflection and how you perceive your past.

For example, you know that this is the final chapter of this book. How does that make you feel? Some people would be excited reaching the final chapter of a long journey, while others may feel a touch of sorrow. It really depends on how you reflect on your past and what you've learned.

For those striving forward in their emotional growth, this is not actually the end of this book. Instead, you will revisit chapters that felt particularly meaningful and read your own words on how this journey has helped you grow. That's what reflection does for us, it teaches new lessons from both our triumphs and our failures.

## DAY 1

> *Pessimism will not get to me! I will remain open-minded at all times.*

### What Makes You Happy?
Can you recall what we talked about in the very first week of this book? If you can't, then that's okay . . . go ahead and cheat by flipping back to Week 1.

While it covered a lot of topics to get us started on the right foot, I am hoping the biggest takeaways were defining what makes you happy—both personally and professionally. Because let's be honest, it's hard to be successful in anything when your personal life is lacking.

So for your journal entry today, I want you to go back to that first chapter and read all of your responses. What made you happy last year? What did you think you were good at? What was your true purpose in life?

Then, I want for you to think about how these things have changed over the past 12 months. Have you discovered new ways to be happy? Has your true purpose in life changed? Did you discover more talents? Write about these developments in your notebook.

## DAY 2

> *Today I will think about my future, where it will take me, and what I need to do in order to get there.*

### Motivation Toward Success

In Weeks 2 and 3 (along with many other parts of the book), we talked about ways for you to find the proper motivation to be successful. This will be different for everyone, and often times, our reasons for striving forward can completely change over time.

So just as you did yesterday, look back at your own personal comments from last year on what motivates you. Then answer these important questions:

**1.** Have your motivations changed for the better over the past 12 months?
**2.** Did you reach any important goals you've been striving for?
**3.** Is it time to re-evaluate your motivations in life to get back on track?

## DAY 3

> *My past has made me who I am today. I am*
> *proud to say that I have failed. That failure*
> *has shaped me into a great leader.*

### Dealing with Failure

A big part of reflection is the ability to understand how to deal with failure. And just so this is perfectly clear, *everyone* fails at some point in life. I think it is a core requirement for being human.

Some of the wealthiest, most successful entrepreneurs in the world today attribute their success to failing. For example, Bill Gates's first business was called Traf-O-Data. It was such a colossal failure that the product didn't even work. They ran out of money and closed the company . . . yet he founded Microsoft only three short years later.

The difference between a successful entrepreneur and someone who feels like a failure in life is how we reflect on those events. So today, your lesson is going to be a pretty difficult one—write in your journal about your biggest business failure to date. Be detailed—this is critically important for your self-growth.

## DAY 4

> *I have been blessed immeasurably. I will remind*
> *myself of those blessings as much as possible.*

### Recognize Your Mistakes

Have you figured out yet how so many of the world's most successful entrepreneurs once failed yet rose to greatness? Well, here's a little secret: there's no such thing as failure.

There's really not. Even the smartest of entrepreneurs will certainly make costly mistakes at times, but they refuse to allow those moments to define them. So instead of admitting failure and giving up, they study these life lessons, recognize their mistakes, and move on with confidence.

For example, Thomas Edison had almost 10,000 inventions that were deemed failures. Yet his response when asked why he kept creating gadgets tells the true story of how to become a great entrepreneur. "I have not failed. I just found 10,000 ways that didn't work."

Today, take some extra time and think about why your biggest business failure occurred. Don't take the easy way out and blame it on a partner, either! Do some real soul-searching and figure out what you could have done to lead to a different outcome. Once you find that answer, write it in your journal.

## DAY 5

> *I refuse to fear failure.*

### Don't Stop Trying

Let's expand a little more on yesterday's lesson and talk about dealing with failure.

For some people, it's like an anchor tied to their legs that keeps pulling them down. No matter how hard they try to shake loose of that sinking feeling, it always seems to prevent them from reaching their goals in life. So they do the easiest thing they can think of—they simply stop trying.

Let me ask you something. Have you truly let go of that failure that you wrote about the other day? Or is it still somehow holding you back or forcing you to play things safe?

Well, today is the day to truly shed any power that memory has over you. So just this once, I'm giving you permission to grab that page and rip it right out of your notebook, and then tear it to shreds by hand. This does not represent who you are as an entrepreneur and it's been holding you back for far too long.

The more pieces you can tear it into, the better.

## DAY 6

> *I shape the world that I live in and I will not allow*
> *anything to change my perception of that world.*

### Don't Forget to Recognize Yourself!

Hopefully you started the day feeling just a little bit lighter now that you're finished dwelling on your past mistakes. That doesn't mean that we're finished with reflections quite yet, though, because I'm sure you've done a whole lot of things right in the past as well.

Can you still remember that amazing feeling you had when you first decided to become an entrepreneur? Every new day felt like a different victory as employees were hired, objectives were met, and profits began to roll in. You did that and so much more, all while shaping a company and inspiring those around you.

Today, I want you to make a list of all your major accomplishments in business. Don't worry, this is not for your LinkedIn profile, so feel free to write the things that you're most proud of in your journal. It doesn't matter whether they were major feats or simply things that brought you a lot of pride. Spend the afternoon reliving these fond moments and how they shaped your career.

## DAY 7

> *When I am faced with failure, I will dig deep*
> *into myself and find a way to overcome.*

### Your Past Defines Your Present

You may have noticed that this has been a particularly difficult week with a few ups and downs thrown in. For that I apologize. At the same time, however, I couldn't think of a better way of ending this book than by having you face both your best and your worst moments as an entrepreneur.

Why?

Think about it for a moment. Your past very much defines who you are as an entrepreneur. In fact, some would say that your combined knowledge and experiences will influence your overall potential in the business world more than any other factor. You use these reflections to make sound decisions, and it's what ultimately makes you a leader.

That brings us to your final task, which we are actually going to divide up over the next several days.

In your journal, draw a line straight down the middle of a fresh page. Then at the heading across the top, write "Strengths" on one side and "Weaknesses" on the other.

Under the "Strengths" column, list every single strength that you have as an entrepreneur. This includes things like your negotiating skills, your ability to delegate effectively, and even things like keeping a healthy work/life balance and rewarding your employees. If you need help making the list, just refer to the chapter titles in this book to give you some ideas.

Under the "Weaknesses" column, do the exact same thing for skills that you're lacking as a business leader. This list is far more important in many ways because admitting a weakness can transform it into a strength if you take the proper actions. Again, feel free to use the chapter titles if you need references.

## DAYS 8–12

*I will lead like a shepherd and encourage my flock to grow.*

### Fast Forward

Over the next few days, pull out your strengths and weaknesses list once again and do a little homework. For each of the strengths on your list, write a sentence on how you are utilizing that skill to motivate others around you, increase your business reach, and/or better serve your customers.

Why are you doing this? Wouldn't it be obvious that you will use your strengths to your favor?

Not necessarily; especially if you're a workaholic who struggles delegating things to others. It is entirely possible that your best talents are not being utilized at all because you're drowning in busywork. This is the perfect opportunity to fix that. Use these next few days to figure out how you can use all of your strengths to your advantage . . . and feel free to glance back at the notes in your journal over the past year for guidance.

And remember, if you have a strength that you're not actively using, then it may as well be considered a weakness.

Do not move to the next section until you have 100 percent finished this research.

## DAYS 13–17

*My weaknesses will make me great.*

### Turn Weakness to Power

Now we're going to spend a few days talking about your weaknesses.

Start going through your list today exactly as you did with your strengths; write a sentence about how you can improve each weakness. This list is a little bit different though because you'll provide one of three answers:

1. If it's a learned skill that you simply won't ever have (like being a great writer or accountant), then write the name of someone you can delegate this task to moving forward. If you don't have a person that can meet that need, then consider looking at an outside company or freelancer to fill that void.
2. If it's a skill that you need to work on, write the chapter of the book where we discussed it earlier and work through those lessons again. If that's not enough to turn it into a strength, then consider private coaching or taking a few classes or seminars on it.
3. If it's a skill that you're pretty good at but simply do not have the time to use, it is not a weakness at all. Move it to the strength category and figure out how to make time to use it to your advantage.

If you take the time to do this for each of your weaknesses, then you become a complete entrepreneur who is ready for virtually anything life can throw at you. Just be sure to follow up with both of these lists from time to time so you're always playing into your strong suits.

## DAY 18 AND BEYOND

### Above and Beyond

Hopefully you've discovered while reading this book that I really tried to go above and beyond with my advice to make you a complete entrepreneur. Words and inspiration can only take you so far though, and the bulk of this journey falls squarely on your shoulders.

Did you keep up with your journal entries? Did you spend sufficient time on the harder assignments to genuinely discover a better path forward?

If you can honestly answer yes to both of those questions, then I am very excited for what your future may reveal. My parting advice to you would be to keep writing in your journal daily, being critical of yourself when necessary; then take the appropriate steps to make real changes. You've been practicing this for a while now and the only thing you're really losing is your daily writing prompts.

So I'll leave you with these parting words: Never stop believing in yourself. Take calculated risks. Inspire your staff. Wow your customers. Give back at every opportunity. That's the only way you'll truly "find your mojo" in business and in life.

Good luck, my friend.

—Rhett

# *Index*

# About the Author

**Rhett Power** cofounded Wild Creations in 2007 and quickly built the startup toy company into the 2010 Fastest Growing Business in South Carolina. Wild Creations was awarded a Blue Ribbon Top 75 U.S. Company by the U.S. Chamber of Commerce and named one of *Inc.* magazine's 500 Fastest Growing U.S. Companies two years in a row. He and his team have won more than 40 national awards for their innovative toys. He was a finalist for Ernst & Young's Entrepreneur of the Year award in 2011 and was nominated again in 2012. He was named one of the world's top 100 business bloggers in 2015.

A member of the U.S. Department of State's International Speakers Program, Power travels the globe speaking about entrepreneurship, leadership, and management alongside the likes of Kiva's Julie Hanna, AOL founder Steve Case, and President Barack Obama. He has written for the *Huffington Post, Business Insider, Time,* and *The Wall Street Journal.*

Prior to founding Wild Creations, Power worked as an economic and small business development consultant for the U.S. Agency for International Development (USAID), serving seven years in the former Soviet Republics of Central Asia. Prior to that he was Director of National Service Programs for Habitat for Humanity International, which included being Habitat's chief liaison with the White House, Congress, and the Corporation for National Service. He now runs a rapidly growing coaching and consulting practice.

Power served in the U.S. Peace Corps and is a graduate of the University of South Carolina. In addition to being the coauthor of *One Million Frogs,* he is a regular contributor to Inc.com and *Success* magazine. He divides his time between Charleston, South Carolina, and Washington, D.C.

**Speaking**
To book the author for speaking or other guest appearances please contact booking@rhettpower.com

**Website**
www.rhettpower.com

"Who can't benefit from a personal coach? Rhett Power's *The Entrepreneur's Book of Actions* can function as your coach, inspiration, and road map for success! This book is a must-read for anyone on their entrepreneurial journey. It's a day-to-day guide that will get you started and keep you going!"

—**Stephen Key, bestselling author of *One Simple Idea***

# THE
# ENTREPRENEUR'S
# BOOK OF
# ACTIONS

# THE
# ENTREPRENEUR'S
# BOOK OF
# ACTIONS

## ESSENTIAL DAILY EXERCISES
## AND HABITS FOR BECOMING
## WEALTHIER, SMARTER,
## AND A MORE SUCCESSFUL
## ENTREPRENEUR

# RHETT POWER

New York · Chicago · San Francisco · Athens · London
Madrid · Mexico City · Milan · New Delhi · Singapore · Sydney · Toronto

1   2   3   4   5   6   7   8   9   LCR   21   20   19   18   17   16

ISBN 978-1-259-85917-5
MHID 1-259-85917-7

e-ISBN 978-1-259-85918-2
e-MHID 1-259-85918-5

This publication is designed to provide accurate and authoritative information in regard to the subject matter covered. It is sold with the understanding that neither the author nor the publisher is engaged in rendering legal, accounting, securities trading, or other professional services. If legal advice or other expert assistance is required, the services of a competent professional person should be sought.
        —*From a Declaration of Principles Jointly Adopted by a Committee of the American Bar Association and a Committee of Publishers and Associations*

**Library of Congress Cataloging-in-Publication Data**

Names: Power, Rhett, author.
Title: The entrepreneur's book of actions : essential daily exercises and habits for becoming wealthier, smarter, and more successful / Rhett Power.
Description: New York : McGraw-Hill, [2017]
Identifiers: LCCN 2016037551 (print) | LCCN 2016050233 (ebook) | ISBN 9781259859175 (alk. paper) | ISBN 1259859177 | ISBN 9781259859182 () | ISBN 1259859185
Subjects: LCSH: Success in business. | Success. | Entrepreneurship.
Classification: LCC HF5386 .P76185 2017 (print) | LCC HF5386 (ebook) | DDC 658.4/09—dc23
LC record available at
https://na01.safelinks.protection.outlook.com/?url=https%3A%2F%2Flccn.loc
.gov%2F2016037551&data=01%7C01%7Ckari.black%40mheducation.com%7Cc
3f3409e16e04fb57f0c08d4027815af%7Cf919b1efc0c347358fca0928ec39d8d5%7C1
&sdata=uJNWHmejO15L26TWZvZ7%2B8%2F2uOrMaICllUJ%2BQ86Bk78
%3D&reserved=0

McGraw-Hill Education books are available at special quantity discounts to use as premiums and sales promotions or for use in corporate training programs. To contact a representative, please visit the Contact Us pages at www.mhprofessional.com.

*Thanks to my family for your constant support.*
*To my boys . . . never let anyone tell you can't achieve something*
*and never stop fighting for what you want in life.*